FREEDOM FROM
(ERVI(AL
AND
BACK PAIN
—THE NATURAL WAY

Er. M. K. Gupta

PUSTAK MAHAL®

Publishers
Pustak Mahal®, Delhi

J-3/16 , Daryaganj, New Delhi-110002
☎ 23276539, 23272783, 23272784 • *Fax:* 011-23260518
E-mail: info@pustakmahal.com • *Website:* www.pustakmahal.com

Sales Centre
10-B, Netaji Subhash Marg, Daryaganj, New Delhi-110002
☎ 23268292, 23268293, 23279900 • *Fax:* 011-23280567
E-mail: rapidexdelhi@indiatimes.com

Branch Offices
Bangalore: ☎ 22234025
E-mail: pmblr@sancharnet.in • pustak@sancharnet.in
Mumbai: ☎ 22010941
E-mail: rapidex@bom5.vsnl.net.in
Patna: ☎ 3294193 • *Telefax:* 0612-2302719
E-mail: rapidexptn@rediffmail.com
Hyderabad: *Telefax:* 040-24737290
E-mail: pustakmahalhyd@yahoo.co.in

© **Author**

ISBN 978-81-223-0104-5

9th Edition : 2009

Printed at : Param Offsetters, Okhla, New Delhi-110020

Preface

There is no permanent cure in Allopathy for chronic diseases like Cervical pain, Backache etc. One can only take some medicines and painkillers to subside his pain temporarily only waiting for its reappearance again with more intensity. This is because this type of treatment only provides symptomatic relief and doesn't remove the root cause of the problem.

Yoga comes to the rescue at such moments and can provide permanent relief if one has patience to pursue it regularly with interest. By maintaining good postures, performing loosening and strengthening exercises for muscles, one can restore the muscles and spine in their proper tone and alignment provided they have not undergone degenerative and irreversible structural changes.

I have tried to the explain scientifically various aspects related to the causes and prevention/cure of these pains so that readers will be fully aware of what and why they are practising. I will appreciate any suggestions/comments from the readers and apologize for any mistakes if left out inadvertently.

Wishing the readers all the best in their endeavour to overcome these unpleasant pains.

New Delhi

—Er. M.K. Gupta
Inter-University Accelerator Centre
(Formerly Nuclear Science Centre)
Aruna Asaf Ali Marg
Near Vasant Kunj
New Delhi-110067
Tel.: 26892601, 26892603
E-mail: *mkg@iuac.ernet.in*

Contents

1

Introduction

Backache and cervical pain are the gifts of modern civilization, which is characterized by a sedentary life, improper food habits, wrong postures coupled with a lot of mental tension. The result is before everybody to see in the form of psychosomatic diseases, foremost among them are backache and cervical pain. It appears that 75% of our adult urban population is suffering from it to a lesser or higher degree.

There are two kinds of backache and cervical pain. One is due to muscle spasm which is responsible for 90 percent of backache & cervical pain prevalent in our society. The other kinds of backache and cervical pain are due to some physical injury to the spine by accident, sudden falling or by some abrupt movement of the body or due to some structural defects or degenerative changes developed in the spine e.g. derangement of the spinal vertebra, arthritis of the spine, slipped disc or scoliosis (lateral curvature of the spine). For all these, specialised medical treatment should be sought. Some of the degenerative changes developed in the spine due to previous carelessness and ageing process are irreversible.

But most back and cervical problems are simply due to muscular tension and tightness, which come from poor postures, overweight, inactivity, weak muscles of back, neck and abdomen. The present book is mainly devoted to such type of backaches and cervical pain only. It covers both preventive and curative aspects of these problems.

However two special chapters on 'Cervical Spondylosis' and 'Slipped Disc' have been included in the book to take care of those cases which haven't reached to a very advanced or chronic stage. The minor structural defects and misalignment of the spine can also be corrected by the practice of good postures and exercises given in this book. The book explains the matter with as much sketches as possible so as to be easily understood by the readers.   OOO

Structure of the Spine

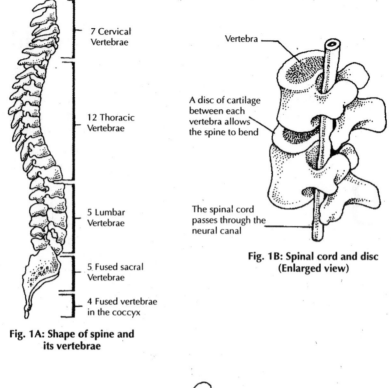

7 Cervical Vertebrae

12 Thoracic Vertebrae

5 Lumbar Vertebrae

5 Fused sacral Vertebrae

4 Fused vertebrae in the coccyx

Vertebra

A disc of cartilage between each vertebra allows the spine to bend

The spinal cord passes through the neural canal

Fig. 1B: Spinal cord and disc (Enlarged view)

Fig. 1A: Shape of spine and its vertebrae

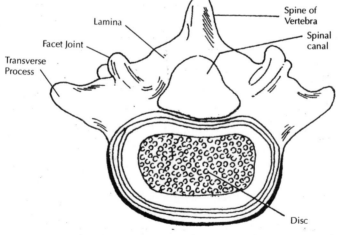

Lamina

Facet Joint

Transverse Process

Spine of Vertebra

Spinal canal

Disc

Fig. 1C: Enlarged cross sectional view

2

General Description of the Human Spine and Back

B efore going into the techniques for removal of backache
and cervical pain, it will be worthwhile to have a brief
knowledge about the structure of the spine and
musculature associated with it, because these problems are
basically related to the spine and associated muscles.

Our spine or backbone consists of 33 small bones called
vertebrae sitting one over the other and separated from one
another by elastic discs called intervertebral discs (see Fig. 1A
& 1B on page 8). The vertebrae are held in place by various
muscles, ligaments and bony processes. Because of the large
number of vertebrae joined together by resilient discs,
considerable movement is possible at the spine. A layman may
ask as to why the spine is not designed as a single rigid piece
of bone. The answer is obvious. It will grossly curtail our
movements in various directions which we can now do with a
flexible spine. But even with so many vertebrae, the spine has
been designed as a stable and cohesive unit so that it is not
easy for the displacement of one vertebra over the other.

Another interesting feature which the human spine has got is
that it has four curves in it (see Fig. 1D). We have one forward
curve in cervical region, one backward curve in thoracic or
dorsal region, again a forward curve in lumbar region and again
a slightly backward curve in sacrum and coccyx region.
Cervical spine has seven vertebrae, thoracic spine has got
twelve, lumbar spine has got five vertebrae (see Fig. 1A). In
sacrum five vertebrae are fused together to form a single, broad,

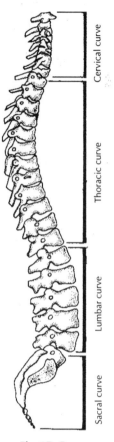

Cervical curve

Thoracic curve

Lumbar curve

Sacral curve

Fig. 1D: Four curves in the Spine

triangular structure. Coccyx, the lowermost part of the spine is formed by the fusion of four very small vertebrae. Some muscles have attachment to this part of the spine also. Out of all these regions of the spine, cervical spine is quite flexible so that you can move your head backward, forward, or from side to side, or turn it. Thoracic spine has got little flexibility. A little movement occurs in this region only during rotation or twisting of the spine. Lumbar spine is again more flexible. Forward/backward movement of the trunk, sideward bending and twisting movement of the trunk — all these basically involve the movement at the lumbar spine.

A layman can ask why there are so many curves in the spine; couldn't it be designed as a totally vertical thing so that load passes axially through this to the legs below? Again these curves have got an important purpose. With these curves and intervening discs, the spine acts as a coiled spring which enables it to absorb the shocks and impacts coming from the ground through the legs more effectively. Without these shock-absorbing properties, the impact of shocks will reach the brain and damage it.

Whenever these curves are disturbed beyond their natural curvatures, unequal pressures and strains are caused on muscles and ligaments associated with the spine which lead to backache and cervical pain. For example when you sleep on a soft bed, the entire curvature of the spine is disturbed. By using a thick pillow you disturb the curvature of your cervical spine. Similarly when you sit slumping or with rounded back on a chair, you disturb the natural curvatures of the spine. All this create unnecessary strain on the spine and associated muscles and

10

ligaments. Infact the central emphasis on back management is correcting the various curvatures of the spine and bring the spine in its correct straighter posture. It is to be noted that curvatures of the spine are required to be maintained during our sleep also. That is why hard bed is recommended. This is the position of maximum relaxation for the spine. It is not expected during sleep that these curves should disappear and your spine should freely sag in mattress.

Now why these curvatures are disturbed? There are many reasons for it; chief among them are — poor postures and weakness of muscles associated with the spine. *There are mainly four groups of muscles which work together to support the spine, they are — the back muscles (erector spinal muscles), abdominal muscles (rectus abdominis), lateral muscles* at the sides of the trunk and the *hip muscles.* Hip muscles have four groups of muscles which work together as one unit namely, *hip flexors (psoas muscles)* located at front of the hips, *hip adductors* located at outer sides of hip, *hip abductors* located at inner sides of the hip (groin), *hip extensors* — the massive muscles at the back of the hip, most important being *gluteus muscles* (see appendix for the diagram of these muscles at page 122).

If any of these muscles is weak or is either too short or too long, the spine will not be in proper alignment and will not rest on pelvis centrally. For example, when abdominal muscles are weak (which is normally the case), the pelvis is tipped forward and the hollow in your lower back (lumbar curvature or lordosis) is increased. This causes the back and psoas (hip) muscles to overwork which creates spasm in these muscles leading to pain in the back.

Muscle spasm is a state of sustained muscular contraction which may happen either due to continuous wrong posture or by sudden strain or sprain of the muscle or because of the laxity of other muscles supporting the spine.

If all the muscles associated with the back are in proper shape, and efficiently and optimally working, the spine will be in correct alignment and the pelvis will be held centrally in a balanced position as shown in fig. 3.

11

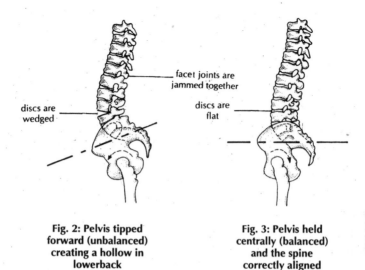

discs are wedged

facet joints are jammed together

discs are flat

Fig. 2: Pelvis tipped forward (unbalanced) creating a hollow in lowerback

Fig. 3: Pelvis held centrally (balanced) and the spine correctly aligned

Now understanding all these, we should conclude that proper movement of the back should primarily consist of the following:

1. Consciously adopting good postures by trying to keep the spine in its 'straighter' posture and pelvis in balanced posture.

2. Relaxing all those muscles which are stiff and in spasm by stretching exercises and to lengthen short muscles and shorten overstretched muscles. A muscle tends to get weaker if it is shorter or longer than its normal size. A muscle becomes shorter if it remains in continuous contraction and gets longer if it remains continuously stretched.

3. Strengthening the weak muscles associated with the spine.

The next chapters of this book are devoted to the discussion of the above mentioned points.

OOO

3

Good Postures to Avoid Backache & Cervical Pain

I n this chapter are given some guidelines about the various types of postures which one should endeavour to maintain during different types of physical activities.

These postures are designed basically on two principles. First is that your spine remains straight (with its natural curves) as much as possible and secondly there is minimum strain on back muscles. Persons with weak back muscles have to be particularly cautious about maintaining these postures because any abrupt movement/bending/twisting/weightlifting can easily cause muscle spasm in the body. The only way to maintain these postures is constant attention and care towards your body position. There is no other way.

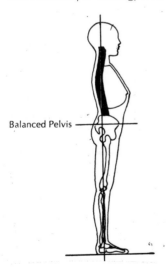

Balanced Pelvis

Fig. 4: Good posture with balanced pelvis

However, it should be kept in mind that in the long run the *maintenance of good posture is a function of strong and supple muscles of the back and abdomen* for which the exercises given in this book should be practised. Unless you strengthen weak muscles and stretch short muscles, you won't be able to attain Ṣpelvic balanceÕ on which hinges your right posture. Please note that bad

13

postures not only cause stress in your muscles and ligaments but can also cause structural changes in your spine at a later stage. The outward visible signs of a bad posture are slumped and rounded shoulders as well as upper back, exaggerated hollow in the lower back and pot belly (abdomen protruding or sagging forward). All this can be eliminated by consciously maintaining good postures and by proper exercises as explained in this book. However, the following general precautions should normally be kept in mind while undertaking any physical activity to save your back from injury:

1. Never remain standing for long.
2. Prefer pulling to pushing the loads and pull with straight arms without bending at the elbows.
3. Don't plunge into strenuous physical activity or exertion or sudden load-bearing without initial warm up and limbering.
4. Avoid sudden bending, twisting of back and abrupt/jerky movements of the body.
5. Don't carry unbalanced loads. Hold heavy objects close to your body.
6. Never lift a heavy object higher than your waist.
7. Don't move or lift very heavy loads. Ask for help.
8. Whenever you have to bend forward, bend from the hip joint keeping your trunk straight. Curving or rounding the back creates stress in the lower back.
9. Don't lift any load while you are bending. Tremendous forces are exerted on the spine and back muscles on lifting a load in the bent position of the back, because of the leverage principle involved in such cases. For correct techniques of lifting load, refer page no. 24.
10. Don't remain continuously in the same postures for long. Change your postures from time to time. If you are sitting for a long time, stand and move around. If you are lying, change sides. Infact no posture is good if you remain in it for long. It leads to stiffness in muscles and stagnation in blood circulation.
11. Remember a general rule that whenever you flex or bend your knees, it reduces the strain on your lower back.

14

This has been explained with illustrations further. Persons with backache shouldn't keep their knees locked and rigid while standing. Keep them loose.

12. Patients with backache should not sleep on the abdomen (prone position). If unavoidable they should place a pillow below the lower abdomen before sleeping or lying in this position. This is to avoid arching in the lower spine which creates strain in the lower back.

Posture 1

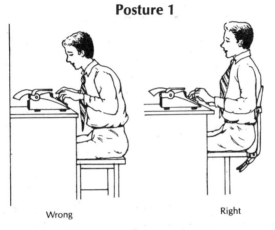

Wrong   Right

Fig. 5: Right Posture while typing

Posture 2

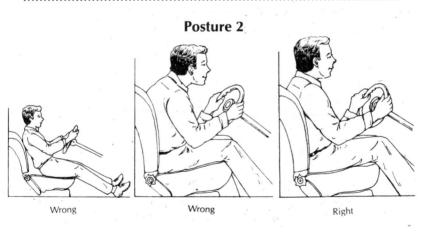

Wrong   Wrong   Right

Fig. 6: Right posture while driving

15

Posture 3

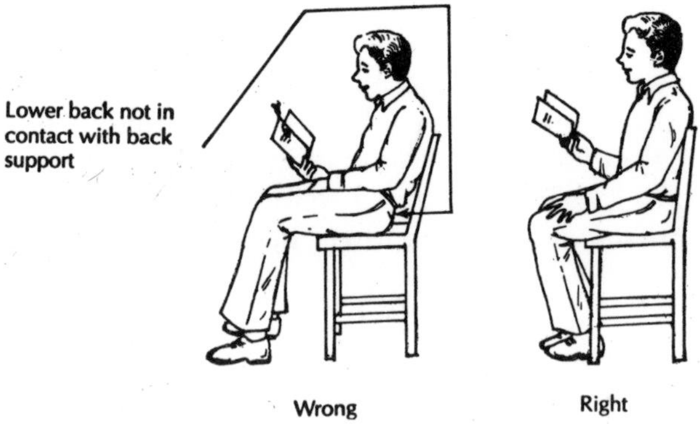

Lower back not in contact with back support

Wrong   Right

Fig. 7: Right posture while reading on a chair

Your lower back should go right upto the back of the seat for proper support. In case you have a long seat and vertical back rest instead inclining by 10-15° (as shown in Fig. 7) then you can't rest your lower back properly against your back-rest. This causes you a great discomfort and back pain. To avoid· discomfort you can put a cushion behind your lower back. Properly designed lumbar support cushions are also available in the market which can increase your comfort of seating in such difficult cases.

While sitting if you have to lean forward on your table due to any reason, always bend from your hips keeping your trunk straight as shown in the Fig. 8.

Wrong,   Right

Fig. 8

Posture 4

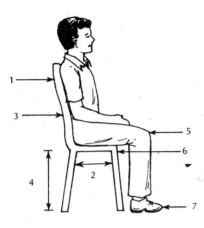

1. Back-rest inclined by 10-15°
2. Depth of seat less than length of the thigh
3. Lower back in contact with back rest
4. Height of chair's seat must be less than the height from knee to foot
5. Knees remain higher than hips
6. Firm and horizontal seat
7. Feet planted flat on the floor

Fig. 9: Specifications for a good chair

Ideally the back of the chair should have a S-curve resembling that of the spine. But in practice it may be difficult. Hence a chair with a straight back inclining at 10-15° from vertical position can be used. However you can provide a lumbar support cushion or normal cushion at the end of the seat to give better support to your lumbar spine. If your chair is already cushioned at the back it is all the better.

If the chair has armrests at the sides, it is preferable. Resting your arms on armrests eases pressure on the back to some extent. Deep seated chair which doesn't allow lumbar spine to be properly supported at the back, must be avoided by the patients of backache. Too much thick cushioning of the seat like a sofa, is also not good. Cushioning should be just sufficient to give you comfort without sagging abnormally on seating.

Posture 5

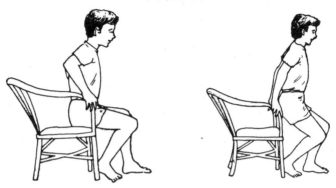

Fig. 10: Getting up from the chair

For getting up from the chair, first slide yourself to the edge of the seat, then have one foot in front of the other and then keeping your back vertical, use your thigh muscles and arms to push yourself to a standing position.

Posture 6

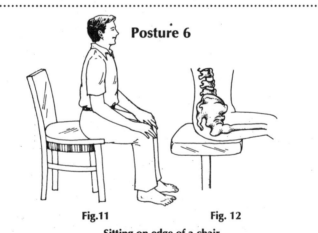

Fig.11   Fig. 12

Sitting on edge of a chair

If it is not possible to sit upto the back of chair, sit on the edge of chair (Fig. 11). This position is called sitting on the 'sitting bones' — the curved ridges of bone at the lower edge of the pelvis. In this position your pelvis and spine are properly aligned and centred and there is minimum strain on back muscles.

18

Posture 7

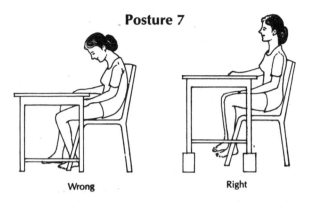

Wrong   Right

Fig. 13: Use a high table to avoid a stoop while at work

To maintain an erect posture and to avoid stooping forward while working, you can also use a slanting board at your table as shown in Fig. 14.

Fig. 14: Using slanting board

Posture 8

Keep your spine straight while sitting on the ground. A cross legged posture helps to keep the spine straighter from the hip upwards. If your back muscles are too weak to maintain it for long, try to sit with your back against a wall with a cushion intervening between wall and your lower back or you can sit with your buttocks slightly raised off the floor on a cushion while keeping

Fig. 15: Right posture for sitting on the ground

your feet on the floor. This will ease off the strain in the lower back, or you can also sit in *Vajrasana*. (see Fig. 113, page 83)

There is a relaxing posture for sitting on the ground as shown in the Fig.15A. This you can try intermittently whenever you get tired with your regular cross legged posture.

Fig. 15 A: Relaxing posture while sitting

Posture 9

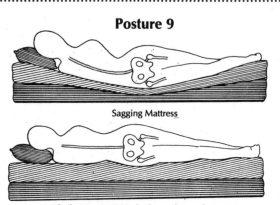

Sagging Mattress

Ideal mattress giving both comfort and support

Fig. 16: Using the right kind of mattress

You should sleep on a firm mattress neither very hard, nor too soft. The body sinks heavily when a person sleeps on a thick soft mattress. The heavier parts of the body sink deeper in bed and the lighter parts stay up. This disturbs the normal curvature of the spine causing undesirable strain on back muscles, ligaments and joints. A straight spine enables the curves of the spine (e.g. lumbar lardosis, cervical lardosis) to remain in an optimum shape which is a position of maximum comfort. That's why a firm bed provides to the spine a posture of maximum relaxation by helping to maintain a straighter posture of the spine.

Posture 10

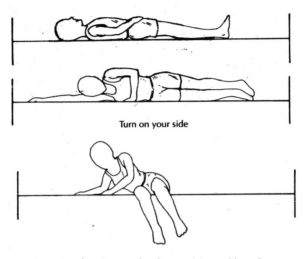

Turn on your side

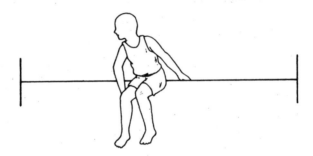

Bend your legs from knees and push up to sitting position using your
arms without twisting or bending the back.

Fig. 17: Get up correctly from the bed

Sleeping on the Back

Persons with a weak back and weak abdominal muscles should lie on the back with knees bent and supported by a pillow or they can place their legs on a small chair. It brings the pelvis to a balanced position which is a position of maximum comfort for the back.

Fig. 18 (a): Unbalanced pelvic position

The pelvis is balanced

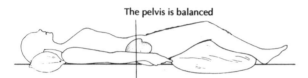

Fig. 18 (b): Knees bent and comfortably supported by a pillow

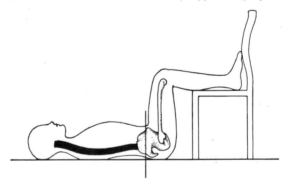

Fig. 18 (c): Balanced pelvic position, legs supported on a chair

Posture 12

Sleeping Position on Side

Patients who have low back pain, should ideally sleep on their side. Some of the recommended positions for side sleeping have been shown below.

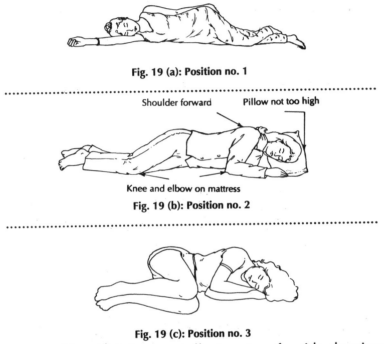

Fig. 19 (a): Position no. 1

....

Shoulder forward   Pillow not too high

Knee and elbow on mattress

Fig. 19 (b): Position no. 2

....

Fig. 19 (c): Position no. 3

Fetus position: This is an excellent posture for side sleeping. Curl up your leg and rest your head on your hands kept one over the other. If you feel your neck straining, put a thin pillow under your hands.

....

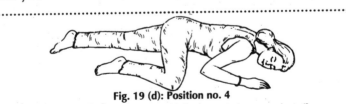

Fig. 19 (d): Position no. 4

The other hand (left hand) will lie straight on the floor with palms towards legs and facing ceiling.

....

Posture 13

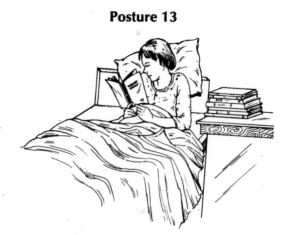

Fig. 20: Reading in bed in an awkward position can cause backache

Posture 14

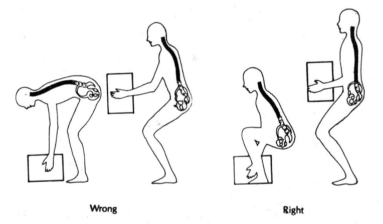

Wrong   Right

Fig. 21: Lifting weights

Most types of backpains are caused by lifting the weights incorrectly. Following steps should be followed while lifting the load:

1. Always face the object you are going to lift. Stand as close as possible to the load with the feet about 45 cms apart. This provides a firm base for lifting the load.

24

2. Now bend the knees and come to a squatting position while keeping your back straight. Grip the object firmly with both the hands.

3. Now stand up straight using the powerful muscles of the legs while holding the load as close as possible to your body by keeping the elbows bent.

Take the following precautions while lifting the load in the above sequences:

1. Don't lift a heavy object higher than your waist or navel level.

2. Don't lift unbalanced and unsymmetrical loads with respect to your body. During a shopping or journey, carry almost equal loads in both the hands. This keeps the spine in alignment. (Fig. 22)

3. Never carry anything that is too heavy with respect to your capacity. Take help of another person and ensure that both of you lift the load symmetrically and put it down together.

Fig. 22

4. Learn to keep your head in line with the spine. Don't tip it forward during the movement.

5. Avoid twisting or bending of the spine while lifting load. Simultaneous bending and twisting of the spine while lifting a load is the most dangerous movement for the spine.

6. Keep the object close to the body. This minimizes the strain on the back muscles.

Posture 15

Handling the Baby

Wrong   Right

Fig. 23

Wrong   Right

Fig. 24

Wrong   Right

Fig. 25

26

Posture 16

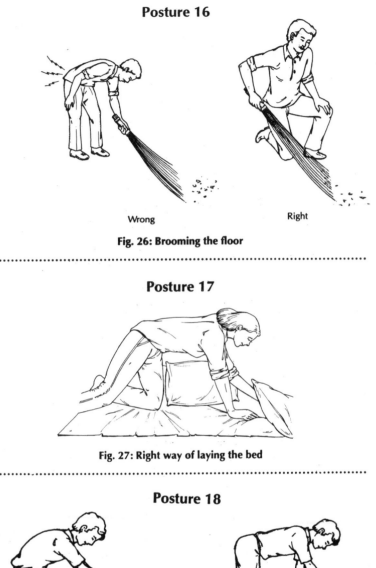

Wrong   Right

Fig. 26: Brooming the floor

Posture 17

Fig. 27: Right way of laying the bed

Posture 18

Wrong   Right

Fig. 28: Mopping the floor

Posture 19

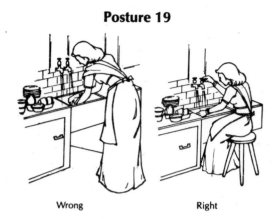

Wrong   Right

Fig. 29: Working in the kitchen

Posture 20

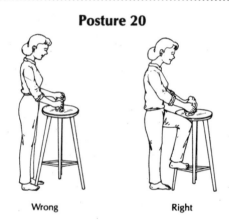

Wrong   Right

Fig. 30: Working while standing

When you have to stand for a long time, keep one foot higher than the other. This reduces strain on the back. The reason is obvious because pelvis is brought to the balanced position by lifting one foot as shown in Fig. 31.

You can keep your foot either on a rail fitted on the table itself or on a separate stool.

Further also keep in mind that while working on a table during standing, the height of the table should be sufficient so that you don't have to bend while working and can maintain the straighter posture of the spine.

28

Some other examples of this type of situation are elaborated below :

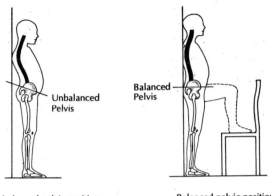

Unbalanced pelvic position   Balanced pelvic position

Fig. 31

1. If you are working on a ladder, put one foot on a rung higher than the other.

2. If you are waiting at a railway station or at an airport, rest one foot on your suitcase. If you have no suitcase or any other luggage, bend one knee and keep the other straight alternately.

3. If you cook while standing, put one foot on a small stool as shown in the Fig. 32. While ironing you can also do the same.

Fig. 32

Posture 21

Fig. 33: Lifting objects at a higher level

When you want to lift an object that is lying at a height, get a stool or ladder so that the level of your head comes to the level of object and you can then take out the object from the shelf in a classical manner with arms bent.

When you lift objects which are above your head, your spine begins to arch which causes strain in your back.

....

Posture 22

Wrong    Right

Fig. 34: Ironing the clothes

Keep the level of ironing board high so that you need not bend.

....

Posture 23

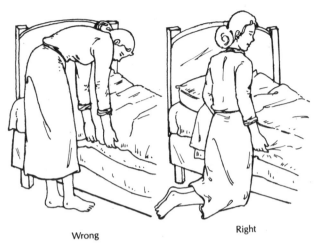

Wrong

Right

Fig. 35: Working on the bed

Posture 24

Wrong

Right

Fig. 36: Don't lay children in sagging cradle

31

Posture 25

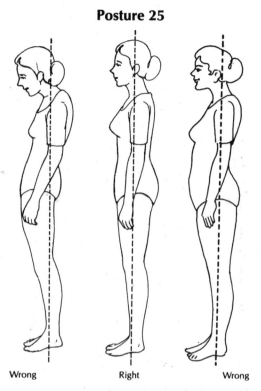

Wrong   Right   Wrong

Fig. 37: Standing postures

To check whether your posture is right or not while standing, draw a plumbline from your ears down. If your body falls primarily behind or ahead of this line, you have a wrong posture. In a correct posture, this line will primarily pass the centre of the body (ears, centre of shoulder joint, middle of hip bone, behind knee cap), finally touching the front of your ankles. You can check it easily while standing sideways in front of a mirror.

The following physical features are indicative of wrong standing postures:

1. Rounded shoulders
2. Upper back protruding backward
3. Excessive hollow in lower back
4. Belly (abdomen) protruding forward
5. Buttocks sticking out abnormally.

However by proper exercises (as are mentioned in this book) and keeping correct postures in various positions, the above mentioned features can be gradually obliterated and the body can be brought to a state of balanced posture.

....

Posture 26

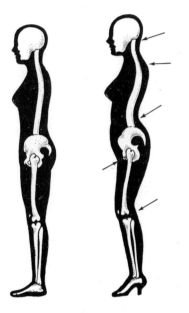

Fig. 38: High heel shoes are not healthy for the back

Your footwear also may cause pain in the neck, upper back, lower back, hips, knees or feet. High heels are not healthy. Choose your shoes carefully.

....

OOO

4

Precautions while Exercising

1. Many exercises have been given in this book. It is not necessary that you do all the exercises. You can select exercises from each section according to the needs and capacity of your body and also those which you enjoy and feel benefitted from.

2. If any exercise causes undue discomfort or pain, stop doing that.

3. Don't do exercises in a painful condition. When pain subsides by any treatment, only then you should gradually start these exercises. This is specially so if the pain is due to swelling or inflammation of the joints, muscles/ ligaments.

4. Where no directions for breathing have been given, breath normally in these exercises.

5. Don't do any exercise upto the limit of pain. Stretch or extend only as much as you can tolerate and increase it gradually with flexibility and strength. Overdoing or overexerting any exercise may harm you.

6. Don't do any exercise as a burden. Enjoy it, and feel and experience the wave of relaxation and well-being arising from it. If you do not feel good while doing the exercises, it means you are not doing it correctly or your mind is somewhere else. Mind and body should move together in an exercise.

7. Wear loose clothes while exercising.

8. Don't start exercises immediately after getting up in the morning. Allow some time for limbering up the body

and muscles by general walking and strolling. Immediately after waking, the muscles are too stiff and you might injure them by sudden movement and jerks.

9. Before doing strenuous exercises do some easy exercises for limbering and warm-up.

10. Do exercises preferably on an empty stomach. The most suitable time will be either in the morning after your natural calls or in the evening when you return tired from office.

11. Duration and repetitions of an exercise should be decided according to individual judgement keeping in mind one's capacity and comfort. As your strength and flexibility increases, you can make corresponding changes in these parameters.

OOO

5

Exercises for Loosening Stiff Neck, Shoulders & Upper Back

Movement of the neck is very much interrelated with the upper back and shoulders. Any movement at any one of these places affect the muscles of others. Hence to really loosen your neck, you will also have to work on the muscles of shoulders and upper back also. In other words unless you remove the stiffness of shoulder joints and upper back you can not really have a free and supple neck. Tension headache, stiff neck, tense shoulders and upper back pain are intimately connected.

The exercises in this chapter aim at making all the muscles associated with the neck, shoulder joints and upper back flexible.

Exercise 1

Inhale and tip your head backwards as far as is comfortable. Try to see the ceiling.

Then tip your head downwards while exhaling, aiming your chin towards the notch in your throat.

Fig. 39

Twist your head towards left trying to look behind. Then twist it towards the right shoulder trying to look behind and keep your chin and head in level while twisting. (See Fig. 40)

Fig. 40

Drop your head first towards the right shoulder and then towards the left shoulder. In order to check alignment of your head is correct while dropping, see that your ear comes close to your shoulder and not any other part while dropping the head. (See Fig. 41)

Fig. 41

All these exercises stretch and loosen the muscles of the neck on various sides. You will benefit more if while bending your neck on different sides you feel the tension that exists on various parts of your neck which gradually gets dissolved by stretching the neck.

Exercise 2

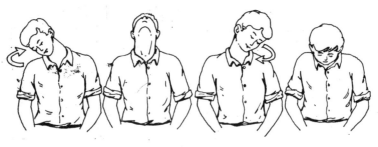

Fig. 42: Neck roll

Sit or stand in to a comfortable position. Very slowly roll your head around into full circle — forward, side, backwards, another side and so on. Do both clockwise and anticlockwise. While you are rolloing your head, you may feel certain tight spots in the neck. You may stop a bit stretching a little at these tight places.

This head roll exercise will loosen your stiff neck effectively and will help you sit with your neck and head more comfortable and aligned.

....

Exercise 3

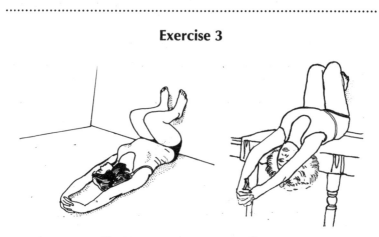

Fig. 43   **Fig. 44**

Lie on your back with your legs on a wall forming an L, with your trunk. Now bend your knees as much as possible with your feet against the wall. This position ensures the safety of your back. Now with your fingers interlocked, take your arms overhead, keeping them straight and firm.

If your breast or pectoral muscles are tight, your arms will not make a complete contact with the ground. With practice, they should be able to lie flat on the floor along their entire length. When they do so effortlessly, your breast muscles are sufficiently long and relaxed.

Now try the same exercise on a table or hard bed against the wall (Fig. 44) with your head slightly jutting out of the edge of the table or hard bed. This provides greater stretch to your front shoulder and chest muscles because arms are able to go beyond 180°.

Exercise 4

Sit on your feet with knees apart on the floor, a few inches away from the wall. Now extend your arms overhead and lean against the wall sliding your hands upwards on the wall. You can also do this exercise by sitting on the edge of a chair or stool. (See Fig. 46)

Fig. 45

Here you use the weight of your body against the wall to lengthen or stretch your front chest and shoulder muscle groups. Don't force, rather let go and relax.

Fig. 46

39

Exercise 5

Interlace your finger and turn your palms outwards. Inhale and stretch your arms up towards the ceiling with palms upward. Hold the position for a few moments. Exhale as you relax and lower your arms to the front. (See Fig. 47)

Fig. 47

....

Exercise 6

Fig. 48   **Fig. 49**

Cross your arms in front of your body and then open them sidewards as you inhale. Without stopping the movement, do it rhythmically exhaling as you cross the arms in front of you and inhaling as you open them on sides. While opening your arms to the sides take them back as much as possible as if you are drawing your shoulder blades together as shown below:

Fig. 50

Exercise 7

Inhale as you raise your arms up and over your head bringing palms together. Raise your heels and stand on your toes and stretch as much as possible upwards. Exhale as you lower your arms to your sides. This exercise puts your whole body in correct alignment, trying to bring every part at its proper posture (in addition to the upper back, shoulder stretch which we are attempting to make.

Fig. 51

Exercise 8

Fig. 52

Inhale and raise your arms overhead, fingers pointing towards ceiling and palms facing forward. Now bend backwards, curving your spine smoothly from tailbone to the top of your neck. Keep the ears between your arms. Make sure your buttocks stay firmly squeezed to avoid any stress on the lower back.

....

Exercise 9

Lift your shoulders up towards ears and then drop them. Do it 5 to 10 times.

Fig. 53: Shoulder lift

....

Exercise 10

Fig. 54: Shoulder circling

Place your fingertips on your shoulders. Bring your elbows together in front of your chest, then lift them as high as possible, keep them together for as long as possible. Direct them back and then begin to lower them behind you. Squeezing your shoulder blades together, lowering your elbows as far as possible, bring them forward and together.

Continue moving in this way making the biggest possible circles with your elbows. Then reverse the direction of movement.

This exercise is wonderful for undoing tension throughout your upper body especially shoulders, upper back and chest.

Exercise 11

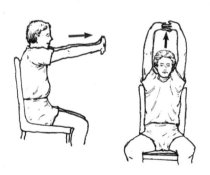

Fig. 55

Interlace your fingers, then straighten your arms out in front of you with palms facing out. Feel the stretch in your shoulders, middle of upper back, arms, hands, fingers and wrist.

Now take your arms upward above your head with palms facing the ceiling. Stretch your arms up and back as much as possible and feel this stretch extending from the shoulders and upper back to the end of the arms.

You can do this exercise both while sitting or standing.

Exercise 12

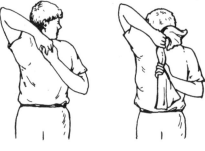

Fig. 56   Fig. 57

Reach behind your head with your left hand as low as possible and grab the fingers of your right hand coming up. Hold the stretch for some time.

If your hands don't meet take the help of a towel (Fig. 57) and try to bring both hands as near as possible. Work a little on it everyday until your hands start touching. Try to keep your posture straight while doing these stretches.

Shoulder stretching is good for reducing tension and increasing flexibility of the shoulders and upper back.

Exercise 13

Interlace your fingers in front. Inhale while raising your straight arms above your head, palms facing the ceiling. Exhale while lowering your clasped hands behind your head, palms facing the back of the head, but don't touch it. Feel the squeeze at the top of your shoulder blades.

Fig. 58

Exercise 14

Sit or stand with the trunk keeping straight. Extend your left arm above the head and as much backwards as possible keeping the arm straight. Now do the same with right hand. Now do it speedily with both hands alternately rising and coming down.

Fig. 59

45

Exercise 15

Stand keeping a distance between your feet. Move both your arms in a circle. While moving them in a circle, cross both arms across the front of your body, feeling the stretch in your upper back muscles, then lift the arms above your head and lower the arms behind your body, feeling the stretch in chest muscles.

Do these clockwise and anticlockwise.

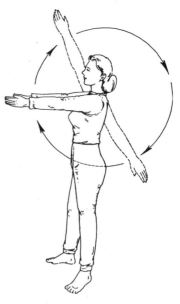

Fig. 60: Arm circling

Exercise 16

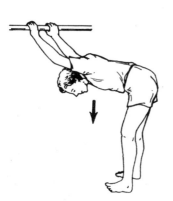

Fig. 61

Place your both hands on a bar or any support and let your upper body drop down freely. This stretch is a very good reliever of upper body tension and effectively stretches your upper back, arms and shoulders and is good to do when you have been sitting slumping all the day.

If you have a parallel bar in your vicinity then this stretch can be done more conveniently by holding both the bars of this device.

Exercise 17

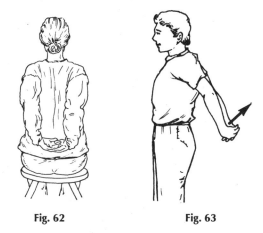

Fig. 62 Fig. 63

Interlace your fingers behind you. Straighten your arms. Draw your elbows and shoulders towards each other squeezing your shoulder blades firmly together. If this is fairly easy then lift your arms behind you (Fig. 63) until you feel a stretch in the arms, shoulders and chest. This stretch is good to do when you find yourself slumping forward from the shoulders.

Another way to stretch the chest and shoulders is to hold on to a support or both sides of a doorway with your hands behind you at about shoulder level. Let your arms straighten as you lean forward.

You can also hold any other convenient support like a parallel bar (if you have one in your vicinity).

Fig. 64

Exercise 18

Interlace your fingers behind your head. Pull your shoulder blades together to create tension in the upper back area. Hold this tension for a few seconds and then release. By first creating tension and then releasing is an effective way to create relaxation.

Fig. 65

OOO

6

Massage for Relaxing a Stiff Neck, Shoulders and Upper Back

Massage is a very effective way for relaxing the tense muscles. It involves kneading, pinching, pressing the tense muscles and then releasing them. This alternate pressing and releasing, rids the muscles of their tension and you experience a feeling of 'let go'. Massage improves the blood circulation in that area and therefore more nourishment reaches to that region making a more effective drainage of waste products and lactic acid — leading to a feeling of increased well-being.

There are some massage techniques which you can do by yourself (i.e. self massage) and in some you may have to take the help of another person. But the most important thing in receiving massage is that you should leave yourself totally loose and relaxed while your partner is doing massage, to get the maximum benefit. Don't tighten your muscles consciously or unconsciously and experience the wavelike feeling of relaxation as your partner's hand moves over your body.

Normally dry palms are used for massage; but if the skin is too dry or if the body is excessively weak, wet cloth or soothing oil may be used. Sesame (til) oil is the best for massage. Massaging is usually avoided during fever and in cases of skin diseases.

Action 1

Grip the flesh at the back of the neck on both sides between your thumb and forefinger and knead firmly. Work up and down from the base of skull to the shoulders.

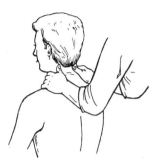

Fig. 66: Kneading the neck

Action 2

Grip the shoulders on both sides of the neck with the heels and fingers of the hands. Knead firmly right from the base of the neck to outer edge of the shoulder.

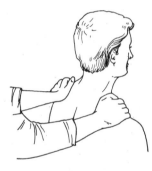

Fig. 67: Kneading the shoulders

Action 3

Use your thumbs to trace deep lines out along the shoulders from the base of the neck. Reach as much deep to the underlying tissues with the thumb pressure as is convenient to the receiver.

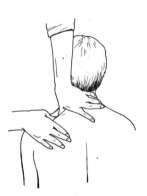

Fig. 68: Deep pressure massage

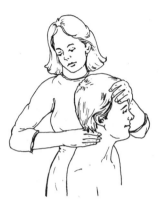

Action 4

Cup your partner's forehead with one hand and use the other to massage the nape of the neck. Pinch the flesh between the thumb and the fingers.

Fig. 69: Massaging the nape

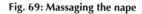

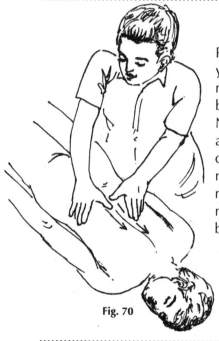

Action 5

Press either side of the spine using your thumbs in a sliding movement from the middle of the back upto the base of the neck. Now a days spine rollers are available which you can just roll over the spine right upto your neck. This movement effectively massages your upper back and neck and relieves your upper body of the accumulated tension.

Fig. 70

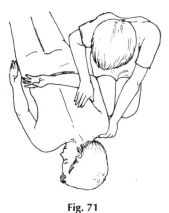

Action 6

Place one hand under your partner's shoulder. With the other hand, work in a deep, pressing circular movement around the shoulder blade, using your fingers. You should be able to feel the movement of the muscles over the shoulder girdle separately.

Fig. 71

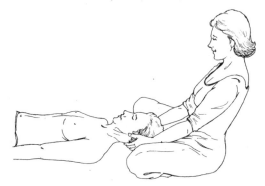

Fig. 72

Action 7

Cup both the hands firmly under the head at the base of the skull. Lift the head a little off the floor and pull towards you stretching the back of the neck (Fig. 72). You can also stretch the neck up and down (Figs. 73 & 74).

Surrender and let go your head to your partner to get the maximum benefit. This is an excellent way to loosen your neck.

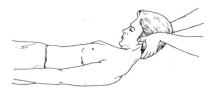

Fig. 73

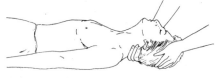

Fig. 74: Stretching the neck

Action 8

Place the palm of your right hand on your left shoulder in the midway, looking towards right. Pick up a handful of skin and muscle and gently begin to knead it using your fingers. **The more tense you are, the tighter your muscles will be.** Now do the same thing on your right shoulder with the left hand, looking towards left.

Fig. 75

Action 9

With your hands grip the shoulder muscles. Tighten and release several times or simply catch these muscles by hands, press your elbows down towards your chest. This movement itself will give enough pressure on these muscles.

Fig. 76

Action 10

This is a very effective way of massaging the upper back, neck and shoulders. Place your hands on lower back. Move them slowly up along the sides of the spine. As you reach the neck,

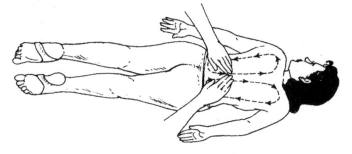

Fig. 76 (a)

separate your hands in a curving movement towards the shoulders and bring them down along the outer edge of torso. While moving the hands, little pressure is to be given by the hands.

....

Action 11

Hacking Massage

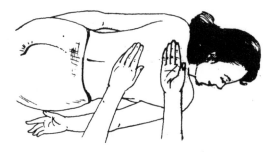

Fig. 76 (b)

Do pounding with the sides of hands on upper back, shoulders and around the neck.

....

Action 12

Vigorously rub and massage the back of neck by the right hand. Work the whole area of the neck right from base of skull to where it touches the shoulders.

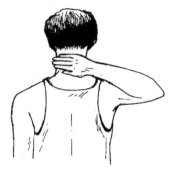

Fig. 76 (c)

OOO

7

Strengthening the Neck and Associated Muscles

Your spine is more vulnerable to injury when the muscles associated with it are weak. Strong muscles keep the spine safe and steady. If your neck muscles are strong, they can hold the cervical spine in a stable position and chances of injuries to the spine by accident or development of structural defects in the spine like derangement of vertebra, inter-vertebral joint displacement are highly reduced.

In this section, therefore, some exercises for strengthening various neck muscles have been described. Some exercises for strengthening the shoulder muscles, upper back and upper arms have also been prescribed because they all supplement the strength of the neck, being interrelated with the muscles of the neck.

Exercise 1

Clasp your hands behind your head. Move your head behind. At the same time prevent it from moving by applying the pressure of hands in opposite direction. Repeat the exercise 4-5 times.

Fig. 77

Exercise 2

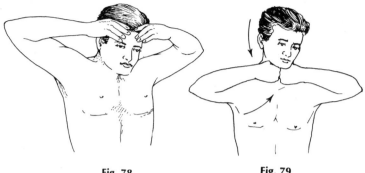

Fig. 78   Fig. 79

Put your hands on your forehead. Bend your head forward. At the same time prevent it from doing so by the pressure of your hands. Repeat it 4-5 times.

You can also do the same exercise by putting your hands below the chin in the form of fists as shown in Fig. 79.

Exercise 3

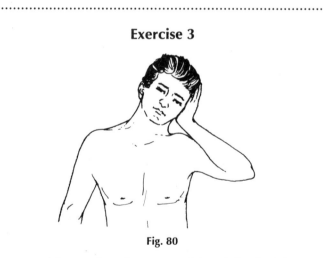

Fig. 80

Place one of your hand on one side of the head. Bend your head to that side. At the same time prevent it from doing so by the pressure of the hand in the opposite direction.

Now do the same thing on the other side of head with the other hand. Repeat 4-5 times on each side.

Exercise 4

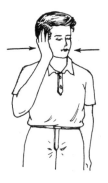

Place your left hand on your left cheek. Try to rotate your head towards left. At the same time prevent it from doing so by the pressure of your hand. Now do the same thing on the other side by placing your right hand on the right cheek. Repeat 4-5 times on each side.

Fig. 81

Exercise 5

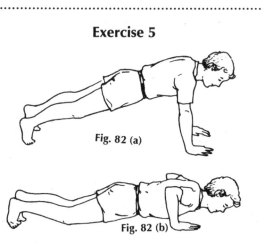

Fig. 82 (a)

Fig. 82 (b)

Fig. 82: Knee push-ups

Kneel down on the ground with all your four limbs. Straighten your legs behind and keep your hands a little more than shoulder width apart. Lower your body straight down until you barely touch your chest to the floor, then push yourself straight upto the starting position. Do it 10-15 times according to your capacity. Keep your knees slightly bent to protect your lower back.

Knee push-ups are very good for upper body development (shoulders, arms, chest, upper back).

Exercise 6

Fig. 83: Seat drops

Catch a steady support with the arms straight and legs placed a little ahead on the floor as shown in the figure. Bend your arms to about 90° or until your hip touches the floor. Then straighten your arms back to the starting position.

This exercise will strengthen the back of your upper arms, shoulders and chest.

OOO

8

Cervical Spondylosis

Cervical Spondylosis is the degeneration (or wear and tear) of the spinal discs in the cervical spine. Cervical spine is made up of seven vertebrae. They are joined to each other by intervertebral discs and ligaments. It is curved with convexity forward. The maximum point of convexity is at the level of disc between the 5th and 6th vertebra. The spondylosis is most common in this disc because this point is the point of maximum stress [Fig. 83 (a)].

In the process of degeneration, disc loses its water and becomes dry. A disc in its healthy state is soft and elastical though strong. Since it is made of elastic fibres it can be compressed and compression of several discs in harmony can produce a smooth bend in the spine whenever so desired.

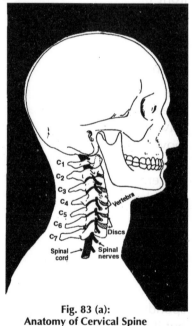

Fig. 83 (a):
Anatomy of Cervical Spine

However, when disc becomes degenerated, its elastic fibres no longer exhibit the elasticity. They become hard and break under stress and the disc gets worn out and thinned. Due to this the edges of the vertebral bodies start rubbing against each other and develop bony spikes called spurs or osteophytes. They are pointed and sharp. They can be seen on the X-rays. If one of these pointed spurs pokes into the nerve root, it causes severe pain in the arm. They can also cause compression of the spinal cord and can produce paralysis in the arms and legs. A degenerated disc can also bulge out of its normal position commonly known as 'Slipped Disc' in which case it can compress a nerve root causing pain. Slipped disc can also occur due to an accident, sudden fall or blow on the neck. (To know more details about anatomy of disc, disc degeneration, disc prolapse, please refer chapter 14.) Movement of the degenerated spine is not smooth as the elasticity of the discs is lost.

Spondylosis occurs normally in the four lower vertebra i.e. 4th to 7th. It rarely occurs in the upper three vertebra mainly because they are not subject to much stress. Pain of cervical spondylosis is always felt behind the neck and never felt in front of neck. When the pain due to Cervical Spondylosis is intense, it can travel down the shoulders and back of the arm upto the elbow joint and sometimes upto hands and fingers. Depending upon which nerve root is affected, the pain will be felt in the corresponding finger.

It is important to understand that the pain of coronary heart disease or angina goes along the inner side of the arm and travels more frequently upto the fingers. Moreover the movement of neck doesn't aggravate the heart pain. But in case of Cervical Spondylosis the pain becomes more by movement of neck. Further heart pain is usually felt on the left side.

Normally degeneration of the discs is an age related phenomena. If an X-ray of the spine is done at the age of 40 years, 30% of them will show degenerative changes and at the age of 50, almost 50% will show evidence of Cervical Spondylosis. At the age of 70, all the vertebras may show spondylotic changes reducing the flexibility of spinal movement but it is not necessary that they will cause pain because nerve root may not have been affected by them.

When a nerve root is affected in Cervical Spondylosis, it can produce the following symptoms:

1. Pain
2. Numbness
3. Stiffness

If a disc slips into the canal and compresses the whole spinal cord, sometimes the paralysis of legs can occur. The compression of the cord can also occur by bony spurs as mentioned earlier.

Treatment

In case of intense pain in the neck due to Cervical Spondylosis associated with or without pain weakness in the arm, usually the following steps may be followed:

1. Stoppage of neck movement: All activities which cause movement of the neck must be immediately halted. There is a lot of vibrations and jerks in the neck during travelling and it is advisable to stop travelling and stay away from the office for a few days.

Fig. 83 (b) : Cervical Collar

A Cervical Collar (see Fig. 83(b)) is advisable to restrict undue movements of the neck. For first few days it is advisable to use collar even while sleeping to avoid inadvertent twisting of neck in sleep. During sleep, the neck should be in 10 to 15° flexed position rather than neutral or extended position. A normal size pillow causes excessive flexion. This should be avoided.

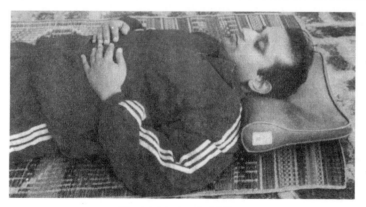

Fig. 83 (c): Cervical Pillow

62

One easy way to support the weak cervical spine while lying is to use Cervical Pillow. (see fig. 83(c))

2. Pain killers: Analgesic is advised to get immediate relief from pain. Very rarely it is necessary to take injectable analgesics. Unless the severe pain is reduced by analgesics, no other preventive or long term measures to treat the disease can be initiated.

3. Heat treatment: Whenever there is pain in the joints, the muscles encircling that joint become tight and reduce the mobility of the joint as a protective mechanism. In fact what nature tries to do through muscle spasm we try to do by wearing a Cervical Collar. When the tension in the muscles becomes too much, they generate pain.

Heat is the best agent to relax the muscles. Many home remedies can be used in this context e.g. hot water bags, electrical heating pads, infrared lamps. One easy way to provide heat to the aching neck is while taking hot shower. Allow shower hot water to fall on the back of your neck while bathing.

The more preferable treatments are Short Wave Diathermy and Ultrasound Heat if they are practically possible by visiting a physiotherapist as they provide deep penetrating heat.

4. Traction: Traction is quite effective when a slipped disc presses a nerve root. Traction increases the intervertebral disc space and therefore the pressure of disc on the nerve root is released. Method of giving traction to neck is shown in the Fig. 83 (d). Traction can be intermittent or steady traction kept up for some time. Stretching the neck as shown in Fig. 72 in this book also serves the same purpose to some extent. If traction fails to

Fig. 83 (d) Traction of Cervical Spine

reduce pain in 24 to 48 hours, there is little reason to insist on its use any further.

5. Massage: Massage is a very effective way for relaxing the tense muscles of the neck as already explained in chapter 5. Various massage techniques have already been explained in detail with illustrations in this chapter.

6. Acupressure: Acupressure on both sides of spine on the upper back is found very relaxing and soothing for the sufferers of pain of Cervical Spondylosis. This acupressure can be given while the patient is sitting or lying in prone position as shown in Fig. 70.

7. Strengthening neck muscles: As already explained spine is more vulnerable to injury when the muscles associated with it are weak. If the muscles associated with spine are strong, the extra load can be shared by the muscles if the spine is weak. Various exercises to strengthen the muscles of neck, shoulders and upper back are explained in Chapter 6.

However these exercises should be taken up only when the initial intense pain is subsided by the conservative treatments described before.

8. Exercises for loosening stiff muscles: After the initial pain has subsided, you can start exercises for loosening stiff neck, upper back and shoulder muscles as explained in Chapter 4.

A few Words about the Surgery

This question is most often asked when a patient should go for surgery in case he is suffering from Cervical Spondylosis.

If a patient has severe pain or significant weakness or paresis or increasing numbness and sensory loss, then surgery is advisable. Similarly if a patient doesn't respond conservative treatment (as described before) for the required number of days, then surgical intervention should be considered. Sometimes pain might get diminished but paresis and numbness remain or get worse. In this case surgery should be considered.

Continued numbness suggests that nerve root is being held compressed to such an extent that its function may soon be lost.

The purpose of operation is to remove all the pressure on the nerve root and the spinal cord, provide more room for both nerve roots and the spinal cord and stabilize the unstable vertebrae by doing a fusion of the two vertebrae by interposing a piece of bone graft in between when necessary. There are a variety of operative procedures. Some are done from behind the neck and some by approaching the neck from the front. The intervertebral disc between two vertebrae is removed and the empty space is replaced by a piece of bone cut to the necessary shape and size to fit exactly into the space created. This extra piece of bone known as bone graft is usually obtained from the patients hip bone (iliac bone). If the spine shows abnormal movement or instability, the logic is to fuse the spine at the level of instability.

Whether operation will cure your problem completely or partially depends upon many things. For example if the numbness is due to compression of the nerve root, numbness will definitely improve but if a nerve is damaged, the numbness will persist even after the operation. It is observed that if the patients come for operation at an early stage whenever such types of symptoms as numbness, weakness in arms and/or legs are found, then the better it is. Delay can produce irreversible changes leading to uncertainty of results in operation. Doing the operation too late merely prevents further damage but can't undo the damage already occurred.

It is interesting to note that only a small percentage of patients are required to go in for surgery Sixty to Seventy percent of the patients carry on well with conservative treatments.

....

OOO

9

Exercises for Loosening a Stiff Back

A stiff and aching back is relaxed primarily by stretching the back muscles which have become tight and thus are causing the pain. Stretching lengthens and relaxes the muscles by releasing the tight pockets. Since hip flexor muscles (Psoas muscles, see Fig. 179, page 123) are closely related with the back muscles and if short in length or in contracted state, they constantly pull the spine not allowing the back to relax, hence hip flexor muscles are also to be stretched for complete relaxation of the back. Exercises in this chapter have been designed accordingly.

It is to be noted that in all the back relaxation exercises, an attempt is made to reduce the hollow of the lower back by bending the knee and the hip joint. Unless this hollow is reduced, back muscles can't be made to relax. More the arch of the spine at the lower back, more stressed and tense the lower back will be. This tension in back muscles occurs in an effort to balance the body position by counteracting the effect of forward pelvic tilt which causes arching or hollow in the lower back. This is why it is always advised to the patients to keep their knees bent and flexed so as to reduce the lumbar curve and thereby avoid the strain in their lower back.

Exercise 1

Fig. 84: The child's pose

Sit in a kneeling position between your feet with buttocks resting between the heels. Keep the head, neck and trunk straight. Relax the arms and rest the hands on the floor. While exhaling slowly bend forward from the hips until the stomach and chest rest on the thighs and the forehead touches the floor in front of the knees. As the body bends forward, slide the hands back into a comfortable position. Don't lift the buttocks off the feet while bending forward. Breathe evenly. As you inhale you will feel the abdomen press against the thighs. Exhaling releases the pressure.

Fig. 85

You can do some variations in this pose e.g. you can interlace your hands behind your back instead of keeping on ground or you can rest your forehead over your hands kept one over the other or you can stretch your hands in front of your head as shown in Fig. 85.

This exercise is excellent for relieving low back pain. It relaxes spinal ligaments, stretches the back muscles and relieves the compression of the lumbar intervertebral discs normally present when standing.

....

Exercise 2

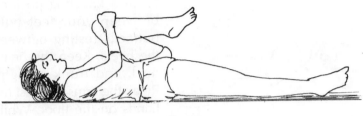

Fig. 86

Lie on your back with the knees bent at about 45° and feet flat on the ground. Bring one knee to your chest, grasp it just below the knee cap and press it firmly against the chest. Straighten the other leg as much as possible. Stay for a while and return to the original position. Now perform the same movement reversing the position of legs.

Fig. 87

You will feel a stretch in the lower back, in back of the thigh of the bent leg (hamstring muscle) and in the front muscles of your hip and thigh of the straightened leg (Hip flexor). This is an excellent exercise for loosening the tired back.

You can also do the same exercise against a wall as shown, which is a more easier version of the above exercise.

Lie on your back, buttocks against a wall and your legs on the wall forming an L with your trunk. From your L position, flex one knee and with your hands bring it as close as possible to your chest. Repeat with the other leg.

Exercise 3

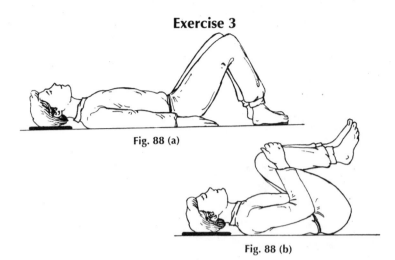

Fig. 88 (a)

Fig. 88 (b)

Lie on your back with a small pillow under your head, your arms at your sides and your knees bent. Now bring your knees up to your chest, and with your hands clasped pull your knees towards your chest. Hold for a count of 10 keeping your knees together and your shoulders flat on the mat. Repeat the pulling and holding movement three times. Relax and repeat the exercise.

Fig. 89

You can also lift your head and touch your knees with it. (See Fig. 89).

You can also do this exercise against a wall which is an easier version of the above exercise as shown in Fig. 90.

Lie on your back, buttocks against the wall and legs on the wall forming an L, with the trunk. Bend your knees, bringing them towards your chest, feet on the wall. Stay in this position as long as you like. It is a safe one. Your back is supported and gravity or the weight of your legs assists the movement. When

Fig. 90

this becomes easy, you can use your hands to pull your knees further.

The above postures are very effective in alleviating severe lower back pain.

....

Exercise 4

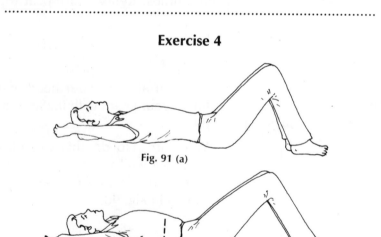

Fig. 91 (a)

Fig. 91 (b)

Fig. 91

Relax with your arms above your head and your knees bent (Fig. 91a). Now tighten the muscles of your lower abdomen and your buttocks at the same time so as to flatten your back against the mat. This is the flat back position (Fig. 91b). Hold the position for a count of 10. Relax and repeat the exercise.

This exercise can also be done while standing as shown below:

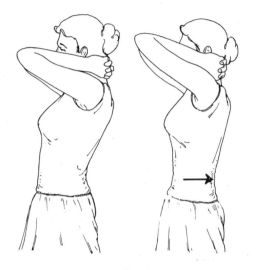

Fig. 92

Stand erect and clasp your hands tight behind your neck. Flatten the "small" of your back by rotating the pelvis up and forward, so as to straighten the lumbar curve.

This exercise relieves tension in the lower back by flattening the lower back and can be done by you on the spot for reducing lower back tightness. This pelvic tilt exercise will strengthen your buttock muscles (Gluteus) and abdominal muscles so that gradually you are able to sit and stand with good posture.

Exercise 5

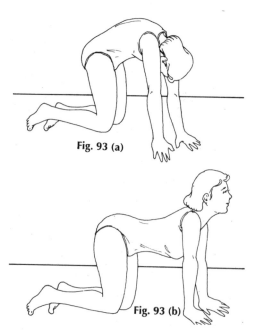

Fig. 93 (a)

Fig. 93 (b)

Fig. 93: Cat stretch

Kneel on the ground on all four limbs. Raise the middle of your back, bending your head downwards towards the ground. Thus your spine will form an arc with convexity upwards. Next lower the middle of your back, raising your head upward towards the ceiling. Your spine will again form an arc with concavity downwards. Repeat these movements 4-5 times.

This exercise removes any stiffness in the spine increasing its mobility and relieves the lower back of its tension very effectively.

Exercise 6

Fig. 94

Fig. 95

Kneel down and sit on your feet (*Vajrasana*). Spread your knees as wide as possible and bring your toes to touch each other behind your buttocks. Then bend forward on to the ground, levering from your hip and keeping the trunk straight stretching your hands as much as possible ahead on the ground (Fig. 95).

Fig. 96

As a variation, you can bend your arms at elbow and rest your head on your hands kept one above the other (Fig. 96).

This is an excellent relaxation pose for the back. It relaxes spinal ligaments, stretches the back muscles and relieves the compression of the lumbar intervertebral discs, normally present when standing.

Exercise 7

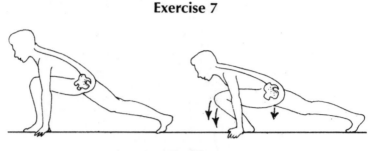

Fig. 97

Lower your body to a squatting position. Place the palms of your hands on ground on either side of your feet. Extend one leg backward as far as possible keeping the left foot on the ground. Lower the front of your hip of the straightened leg downwards to create an easy stretch.

You will feel the stretch in the front of the hip of the straightened leg (Hip flexor muscles) and in the hamstring muscles of the bent leg and in calf muscles of both the legs. Hip flexor is an important postural muscle. When shortened it pulls the pelvis forward and doesn't allow pelvis to reach a balanced position thus creating strain in the lower back. In this exercise hip flexors are stretched relieving the lower back from stress.

Exercise 8

Fig. 98

Place the ball of your foot on a secure support of some kind (table, wall or fence) which is at a height of about $2\frac{1}{2}$' from the ground. Keep the down leg pointed straight ahead. Now bend the knee of the up leg as you move your hips forward. This will stretch your groin hamstring of the bend leg and hip flexor (front of the hip) of the straight leg.

74

Exercise 9

Fig. 99: Squatting

From a standing position, squat down with your feet flat and toes pointed out at approximately 15° angles. Your heels should be 4-12 inches apart, depending upon how limber you are.

Initially if there is a problem in squatting, you can hold onto some support by hand or you can sit with your back against a wall or you can sit on some sloping ground (where it is easier to squat with your face towards the downward side of the slope). All these positions are shown below:

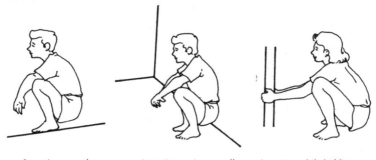

| Squatting on a slope | Squatting against a wall | Squatting while holding |
| | **Fig. 100** | on to a support |

The squat stretches the hamstring muscles of both the legs, calf muscles, groin muscles and the back in particular. Infact the squat is a very comfortable position and relieves any tightness in the lower back.

To stand up from the squat position, raise straight with your quadricep muscles of your legs doing all the work and keeping

Fig. 101

back straight. Don't bend forward as you stand up. This puts too much pressure on your lower back. Now to be able to use **your quadriceps effectively, they have to be strong enough otherwise you are likely to bend your trunk and put pressure on your lower back.** To strengthen quadriceps, the easiest way is to walk up stairs, wherever opportunity is there instead of using lift. Other exercises involve bending your knee partially light and then getting up straight.

It is important to keep your back or trunk straight with the face seeing front in all squatting positions as has been shown by exaggerating the figure for your convenience in understanding.

Fig. 102

Exercise 10

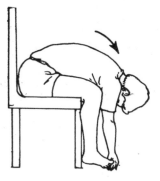

Fig. 103

Sit on a chair, in such a position that your feet are kept flat on the floor. Keep your legs and feet a little apart on the ground because you are going to place your shoulders and arms between them.

Slowly and smoothly bend forward from your hips, allowing your shoulders and arms hang loosely between your legs and feet. Stay in the position for a comfortable period and then return slowly to the sitting position.

This exercise stretches the back muscles and the muscles at the back of the thigh (Hamstring muscles). These are key postural muscles.

Note: In case your chair is not flat (Horizontal seat) or your feet don't rest flatly on the ground while sitting upto the back of the chair, do the exercise while sitting at the edge of the chair.

....

Exercise 11

Fig. 104: Back roll

In sitting position hold your knees with your hands and pull them to your chest. Gently roll up and down your spine, keeping your chin down towards your chest. This will further stretch the muscles along the spine. Try to roll evenly and with

Fig. 105

control. Roll back and forth 4-8 times or until you feel your back starting loosening up. You can also roll by catching your feet or big toe instead of knees as shown above. Back rolls are excellent way for loosening a tight back.

....

Exercise 12

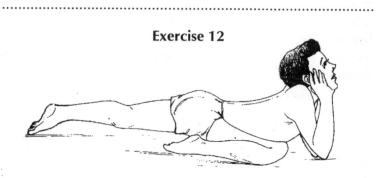

Fig. 105 (a)

Lie in prone position. Bend your one leg and bring it under the chest so that the knee is pressing the chest. Now support your chin with the palms of your hands, elbows resting on ground. Look up, the other leg should remain completely straight.

Now do the same with the position of legs reversed.

○○○

10

Exercises for Loosening the Hip Joint, Hamstring & Calf Muscles

It should be clearly understood that lumbar joints don't act alone but in close relationship with the joints of the hip. If the hip joints are stiff and inflexible, the strain and load of trunk movement usually fall on the lumbar vertebra. The hip joints, being larger and stronger, don't weaken or collapse before the lumbar joints. Therefore, to lessen the strain on the lumbar joints you have to create a better movement and flexibility of the hip joints and muscle groups which operate them. After the hip joints have become reasonably supple, your back will be relieved of quite a lot of strain.

For example, if you bend down to pick up something from the floor, and your hip joints are flexible, you will primarily bend from the hip joints and only secondarily at the lumbar joints. But if your hip joint is locked and unyielding, your back will curve and lead to strain in the lower back. This is because we are making a movement for which our back is not designed. Forward bending of our body is supposed to be mainly by flexion of hip joints maintaining our trunk almost straight. Overbent and rounded trunk are unnatural and strain the body. Once your hip joint is flexible, you will then automatically ease the pressure on your back and therefore avoid unnecessary wear, tear and pain in your lower back which is the most susceptible part of back for occurrence of pain.

The exercises given in this chapter will open your hip joint and will stretch various muscles associated with the hip improving their tone and flexibility. The exercises have also been given to make your hamstring muscles (muscles at back of the thigh) and calf muscles flexible. As a layman, one may ask as to what these muscles have to do with back comfort. But there is a very valid reason. Unless your hamstring muscles and calf muscles are flexible, they will not allow you to bend at your hip joint freely. Even if your hip joint is flexible, still the stiffness of these muscles will restrict your bending beyond a particular point because they won't be able to be fully stretched which is required for this bending.

Exercise 1

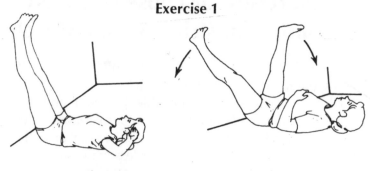

Fig. 106   Fig. 107

A wall is very useful for stretching the groin, while you relax. on your back. Keep your legs elevated on a wall with your hips about 3-4" away from the wall. Slowly separate your legs with your heels resting on the wall until you feel an easy stretch in your groin and inner thigh muscles. Hold the stretch for some time and bring your legs back to the original position.

This exercise effectively stretches your groin and inner thigh muscles (Hip abductors) with the assistance of gravity while you lie fully relaxed.

You can also perform the following variation of this exercise.

Fig. 108

Bring your legs down with soles of your feet together resting against the wall. To increase the stretch further gently push your knees out by your hands.

The wall makes it possible to hold these stretches longer in a relaxed, stable position. Don't stand up quickly after remaining in a leg elevating position. First sit for sometime and then stand up, otherwise you may feel giddy.

You can also use elevated leg position to stretch your neck as shown. Interlace your fingers behind your head and gently lift your head upto a limit of comfortable stretch.

Fig. 109

....

Exercise 2

Fig. 110: Groin stretch while lying

Lie your back with knees bent and soles of your feet together. Try to bring the soles as close to your groin as possible. Let your knees fall apart. Relax in this position for sometime **as you allow gravity to give you a mild stretch in your groin area.**

....

81

Exercise 3

Fig. 111

Keep your one leg on a support at table height keeping it straight. Now while looking straight ahead, bend forward from your hip slowly sliding your hands towards the toes of the elevated leg, till you feel a good stretch in the hamstrings (back of the thigh) of the raised leg. Slowly increase your limit of bending as your flexibility increases. But never curve your back while bending in an excitement to touch your legs with your head.

Do the same exercise with the other leg.

....

Exercise 4

Fig. 112: Hamstring stretch

Lie down on your back with knees bent at about 45° and feet planted on the floor. Bring one knee up towards the chest. Now straighten this leg towards the ceiling. Experience stretch at the back of the thigh (Hamstring) of this leg. Hold on for a while and gradually lower down to the floor keeping it straight without bending and then bring back to original position of the bent knee. Now do the same movement with the other leg and then with both legs. However when you are doing with both the legs, bring them down while bending over the chest to avoid stress on the lower back.

This exercise is designed to stretch the muscles at the back of your thighs (Hamstring muscles). They are key postural muscles and must be maintained flexible for freer movement of your hips and back.

Exercise 5

Fig. 113: Vajrasana

Kneel on the ground and sit between your feet such that the big toes of both the feet overlap each other and the buttocks rest on the inner sides of the feet. Place your hands on the knees and sit erect.

This *asana* automatically aligns your pelvis and spine in their proper shape and makes the whole body steady. It makes your hip joint, knee joint and ankle joint flexible. It stretches some of the articular muscles of your hip by rotating your thigh inwards.

Exercise 6

Fig. 114

Sitting in the position as shown, move your knee of the bent leg up and down rhythmically. You can also push your knee down with the hands rhythmically to have a greater stretch.

Exercise 7

Fig. 115: Groin stretch

Sit on the ground. Bend the legs at the knees and join the soles of the two feet together. Grip your feet with hands and bring them as close to the groin as possible.

Try to keep your back straight and not rounded. Now move your knees up and down in a rhythmic motion. You can also press your knees sometimes with your hands to feel more stretch.

Now lean forward keeping your trunk straight and bending from the hips as much as you can. Head and shoulders should not stoop. They should remain in a straight line with the trunk. Hold this position for some seconds and then come back and relax.

Fig. 116

This exercise stretches the groin and hip adductor or inner thigh muscles and increases the flexibility of the lower back.

Note: Keeping back straight doesn't mean vertical. Back may be inclined with respect to hips but it should not be rounded and should be in a straight line right from the head to the hip joint.

....

Exercise 8

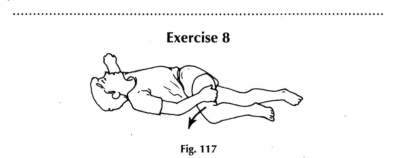

Fig. 117

Bend one knee at 90° and with your opposite hand, pull that bent leg up and over your other leg as shown. Turn your head to look towards the hand of the arm that is straight (head should be resting on floor, not held up).

Now, using the hand on your thigh (resting just above the knee) pull your bent leg down towards the floor until you get the right stretch feeling in your lower back and side of the hip. Keep the feet and ankles relaxed. Make sure the back of your shoulders are flat on the floor. If not, the angle changes between the shoulders and the hips and it is more difficult to create a proper stretch. Hold an easy stretch for 30 seconds, each side.

This exercise stretches the lower back and side of the hip (Hip abductors). If you find it difficult to do. you can do a slightly easier version of it as shown in Fig. 118 and explained below:

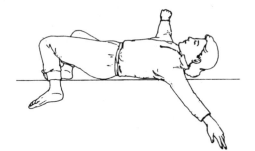

Fig. 118

85

Lie down and bend your knees upto 45° with the feet flat on the floor. Stretch out your arms on both sides. Inhale and then exhaling lower your knees to the floor on your right. If this is painful, then lower them part way. Inhale while raising your knees up again and then exhale while lowering them to your left. Raise and lower them from side to side several times, in synchrony with your breathing.

There is another variation as shown below which you can also try.

Fig. 119

Lying on the back, with both the legs bent at the knees and the arms extended sideways at the level of the shoulders.

Bend at the hips to bring the knees over to the chest, and then by rotation press down to the side with bent knees, the legs jointly against the floor and to a position nearest possible to the extended arm (without moving the opposite side and the lower back from the floor) bring back the knees over the chest and then revert to the starting position. Repeat on the other side.

....

Exercise 9

Place the balls of your feet on the edge of a kerb or stair with the remaining part of the feet free. Hold onto some object for support. Move the heels of the feet up and down and feel the stretch in your calf muscles and achilles tendon.

Fig. 120: Calf muscle stretch

Exercise 10

Fig. 121

Sit with your feet a comfortable distance apart. Slowly lean forward from your hips. Keep your hands out in front of you for balance and stability. This exercise if done correctly effectively stretches your groin and inner thigh muscles (hip adductors).

Don't curve your back round while leaning forward. If your back becomes rounded, it is because your hips, hamstrings and groin are tight which are to be gradually loosened.

Fig. 122: Avoid rounded back while leaning forward

A good way to gradually adapt your hips and lower back to a proper, upright position is to sit with your lower back flat against a wall.

Fig. 123

Another way is to sit with your hands behind you. Using your arms as a support will help lengthen your spine.

Fig. 124

After your lower back and hip have become a little flexible, you can do the following variation also in which you bend towards each leg separately to stretch hamstring muscles of the legs and opposite side of the back.

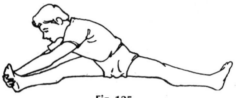

Fig. 125

If this is difficult, bend one leg at the knee and put its sole at the inner thigh of the opposite leg and then bend as shown in the following figures.

Fig. 126

Fig. 127

Exercise 11

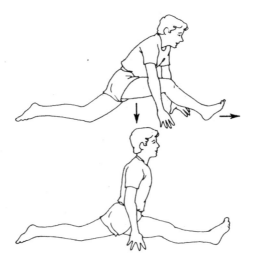

Fig. 128: Split

Kneel on the floor with all the four. Slowly move your front foot forward until you feel a controlled stretch in the back of the legs and groin. Think of your hips going straight down. Use hands for balance and stability and keep your back vertical. Gradually you should be able to move your front foot farther and farther till your hip touches the floor. Be sure not to overstretch.

Exercise 12

Fig. 129: Side Split

From a standing position, gradually spread the legs until you feel a stretch on the inside of your upper legs. Think of your hips going straight down. Use hands for balance. As you become more flexible, you will be able to move your feet more apart. As you get lower in this stretch, you can allow your toes off the floor with only heels touching the floor.

Splits increase the flexibility of your hip joints considerably, but they should be tried only after you have become reasonably flexible by other simple exercises.

....

OOO

11

Exercises for Strengthening the Abdominal Muscles

Abdominal muscles provide support to the front of the spine besides supporting the abdomen. When the abdominal muscles are weak, the abdomen bulges outwards alongwith abdominal contents. This pulls the pelvis forward and causes pelvic tilt and exaggerated hollow in the lower back causing pain and tension in the lower back.

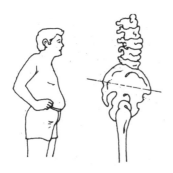

Fig. 130   Fig. 131
Pelvis tilted forward

When abdominal muscles are weak, the other muscles that control the back, mainly back muscles and hip flexors (psoas muscles) have to overwork to maintain the balance. This is what results in pain, discomfort or even spasm. If no precaution is taken, our abdominal muscles gradually become permanently lengthened and flabby because of a sagging abdomen.

In fact, weak and flabby abdominal muscles are the main culprit for a bad posture and back discomfort. If your abdominal muscles are strong, the tendency of the pelvis to tilt forward and down is automatically prevented and your pelvis remain in a balanced position without causing undue strain on the back muscles.

The exercises in this chapter aim at strengthening your abdominal muscles.

Exercise 1

Fig. 132

Lie on your back with knees bent and feet flat on the floor. Put your hands on your chest or interlace them behind your head. Now lift your head and shoulders off the floor so that your upper body is curled forward upto about 30° from the floor. Stay in this position for a while and then come back slowly.

This exercise strengthens your upper abdominal muscles.

Exercise 2

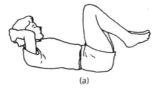

(a)   (b)

Fig. 133

Lie on your back with knees bent and feet flat on the floor. Interlace your hands behind your head. Now raise your bent legs off the floor and try to bring the knees as close to your chest as possible. **This exercise strengthens your lower abdomen.**

Now keeping your legs in the same position, also lift your upper body from the floor and try to touch your elbows to the knees by rotating your arms inwards. **This posture strengthens both your upper and lower abdomen.** Stay in this position for a while and then come back slowly.

You can do a small variation of this exercise while you are in a posture as in Fig. 133 (b), straighten out your legs and hands as shown in Fig. 134.

Fig. 134

Remain for a while in this pose and come back.

....

Exercise 3

Fig. 135: Leg Slide (Cycling)

Lie down on the ground with knees bent at about 45° and feet planted on the floor. Draw the right knee towards the chest and at the same time, move the left leg away from the body without touching the ground (a little up from the ground). Now reverse the roles of the legs. The movement will resemble cycling, continue for some time.

This exercise strengthens abdominal muscles and at the same time strengthens leg muscles and stretches the back also.

....

Exercise 4

Fig. 136

Lie down on your side with one hand supporting the head and the other placed flat on the ground for balance. Ensure that your trunk and legs remain in one straight line. Slowly raise the upper leg as far as possible towards the ceiling. Hold for a while and then slowly return the leg to its original position. Do it 4-5 times. Now repeat the same procedure lying on the other side. Do the exercise while keeping the abdominal and buttock muscles firm to keep your pelvis and spine in correct alignment.

This exercise strengthens the muscles at the sides of the trunk which are one of the postural muscles to keep your spine steady.

Exercise 5

Tighten your stomach muscles and pound it by the closed fists of your hands. It strengthens your stomach muscles.

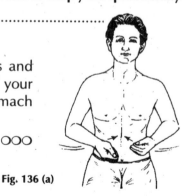

OOO

Fig. 136 (a)

12

Exercises for Strengthening the Back Muscles

Weakness of the back muscles is one of the major cause of Backache. The reason being that weak muscles easily come in spasm even with little strains on them. Whenever they are expected to take some additional stress either due to poor posture or due to sagging abdomen and forward pelvic tilt or due to physical exertion or lifting and moving some object, they develop spasm (or sustained muscular contraction) because of their inability to bear these stresses. Muscles which are strong can even nullify the other precipitating factors for the backache.

Because of continuous contracted state, the small blood vessels that supply nutrients to the muscles or that drain away waste products are squeezed shut. It is because of such accumulation of waste products and cutting off the nutrition that muscles in spasm become very tender and painful. Muscle which remains contracted for a long time, first tires and then hurts.

There are some exercises for strengthening weak muscles of the back. However before attempting such exercises, muscular tightness should first be removed by stretching and relaxation exercises as mentioned in the earlier chapter. The muscles associated with the back should be restored to their optimal working lengths. This would ultimately strengthen the weak muscles and lengthen short muscles.

Exercise 1

Fig. 137: Cobra pose

Lie face down with your legs together. Place your hands flat on the floor on either side of your chest. Inhale while raising your upper body upto your navel using primarily your back muscles and only secondarily using your hands. Look towards front. Hold for a while and then come back gradually while exhaling.

This exercise strengthens your upper back muscles.

Exercise 2

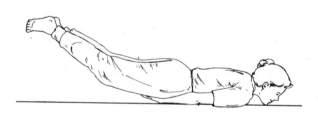

Fig. 138

Lie down on your stomach with arms by your side. Keep your palms underneath your thighs. Inhale and slowly raise one leg off the ground keeping it straight upto your comfortable limit. Hold for a while and then lower it down slowly. Do the same movement with the other leg and then with both legs simultaneously.

This exercise strengthens your lower back and buttock muscles.

Exercise 3

Fig. 139

Lie down on your stomach with the arms extended above your head. Inhale slowly and smoothly and raise the upper body along with the arms and legs off the ground upto your comfortable limit. Hold this position for a while. Then slowly lower down to your original position.

This exercise strengthens the muscles of your buttocks (gluteus) and the entire back.

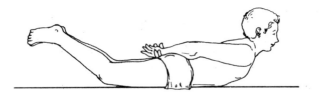

Fig. 140

If you find this exercise difficult to do with your hands stretched overhead you can interlace your hands behind your hips and then do the exercise as shown in Fig. 140. Gradually as your strength develops, you can do the earlier posture.

Exercise 4

Fig. 141

Kneel on the ground on all the four limbs as shown. Lift one leg and extend it backwards. Revert to the starting position and do the same with the other leg. Do 4-5 times with each leg.

This exercise can also be done in standing position. Hold some support by hand at your shoulder level and then lift one leg as high as possible. Now do with the other leg.

....

Exercise 5

Fig. 142

Walk around the room keeping the knees and elbows straight ensuring that feet lie flat on the floor. It strengthens the back and abdominal muscles.

....

OOO

13

General Exercises for a Flexible and Healthy Spine

The spine is able to move in four directions: forward, backward, sideways and in rotation and it should be moved regularly in all four directions. Potentially the spine is extremely mobile but lack of movement and tightened muscles quickly cause it to stiffen and lose its mobility and elasticity. Its restricted capacity for movement also hampers you in your daily activities and increase the risk of injury if you have a minor accident or lose your balance. The postures of classical *yoga* concentrate almost exclusively on the spine and include always these four types of spinal movement.

Practising these movements will also increase circulation to the spinal nerves, so that you will feel generally better and more energetic. The spine is also an energy channel. For subtle energy (*Prana*) to flow freely through it, it needs to be maintained in a healthy, flexible condition and above all it needs to be held erect. Infact it is said that a flexible spine is the sign of youth.

Many medical practitioners use the method of 'spinal manipulation' in the treatment of backache which establishes the importance of a healthy spine. Manipulation of spine involves various pulls and thrusts, upon the spine. But since 'prevention is better than cure', we should maintain a flexible spine rather than correcting disordered one.

Exercise 1

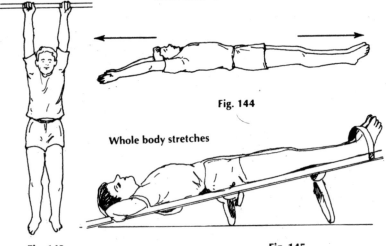

Fig. 144

Whole body stretches

Fig. 143   Fig. 145

These whole body stretches are very good for stretching and relaxing the whole body right from toes to your arms and bringing it in correct alignment. They stretch your arms, shoulders, chest, upper and lower back, abdomen, hip, legs and feet. They also help in the correction of lateral curvature of the spine or any antisymmetry in the body.

In Fig. 143, you stretch the body by hanging on a bar. In Fig 144, you put your hands over your head while lying down and pull your arms and legs in the opposite direction. In Fig 145 you lie on a slant board with your feet elevated and anchored in the strap at the end of the board. There is nothing to do now. Just lie relaxed and allow gravity to stretch your body.

Exercise 2

Fig. 146: Backward bending   **Fig. 147: Forward bending**

Inhaling, stretch your arms upward and backward and bend your spine back. Exhaling, come back up and then bend forward from your hip keeping the trunk straight, as far as you can. Repeat this forward/backward motion, inhaling as you go back and exhaling as you come forward. Gradually increase the speed. You can also swing your arms right-left while you are hanging loosely in a forward bending position.

Exercise 3

Fig. 148

Inhale and raise your arms to the sides up above your head. Straighten your elbows, interlace your finger and turn your palms to face the ceiling. Exhale as you stretch over to right. Keep your arms straight touching your ears, your shoulders well back and your buttocks and abdomen firm. Curve smoothly and maintaining your axis without swaying either forward or backward. Inhale as you slowly come back to the vertical position. Now do the same movement on the other side.

These movements increase the flexibility of the spine in lateral direction and also stretch the abdominal muscles lying on the sides of the trunk.

Exercise 4

Fig. 149: Twisting

Stand with your feet 60 cm. apart and your arms spread out horizontally. As you exhale, twist to the right and extend your right arm back, bending your left arm at the elbow and looking behind. Keep your body straight. Inhaling, turn to the front, and now twist to the left. Repeat many times, gradually increasing the speed and breathing rate.

OOO

14

Treatment for Slip-Disc and Sciatica

Anatomy of Spinal Discs

Before going into detailed discussion of the Slip-disc treatment, first we should properly understand the anatomy of disc and vertebra.

Discs are cushions of cartilage that separate any two vertebrae. They are very tough yet flexible structures. They act as shock absorbers getting compressed when weight is put upon the spine and springing back to their original shape when the weight is taken away. Disc dampens the force which comes from your feet when you walk or run so that it doesn't go to the brain to cause damage. Discs all together constitute about one third of the total length of the spine. It is because of these elastic discs that you are able to bend your spine in many directions (flexion, extension, rotation, lateral bending).

This disc absorbs water, becomes taut and packs the joint to act as a wedge between the vertebra. When the discs are fully hydrated with water and firm, they are effective wedges, particularly in the lumbar region reducing the demand on the back muscles. If the discs are not fully hydrated and their wedge quality is poor, it becomes the increasing responsibility of the back muscles to keep the body upright.

During the day, when you are upright and moving, the force of your weight in motion (which is more than your static weight) will force water out of your discs and into the vertebrae above and below. This release can cause a shrinkage in height of about one and half to two centimeters during 12 hours. During the night, while you sleep, the discs absorb water from its surroundings. Disc has no blood vessels and nerves of its own. There must be enough free water in the region for it to be able to rehydrate itself. Hence the importance of more water intake for those who have a tendency of low back pain. Bed rest recommended in treatment of disc problems prevents shrinkage of discs and allows full rehydration of the discs. Incidentally, in the case of astronauts travelling in space, the discs swell considerably due to weightlessness in space and the height of astronauts increase as much as two inches.

The disc is composed of an outer fibrous material called 'Annulus fibrosus' and an inner pulpy substance called 'Nucleus pulposus'. It is the property and function of the pulpy substance of the disc to absorb or give up its water. The fibrous part firmly fixes the disc to bony edges of the vertebrae.

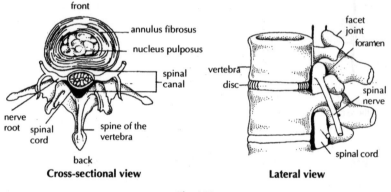

Fig. 150

Cross-sectional view   Lateral view

Degeneration of Spinal Discs

With the advancement of age, thinning and degeneration of discs including general wear and tear of spine takes place and it starts in everybody from the age of 25 to 30 years. By the age of 60 years, it is quite advanced. With the degeneration of the disc its load bearing capacity decreases and spinal movement at that level is restricted. When disc is completely degenerated, it is like a lifeless mass and can't be regenerated. Slip disc is invariably associated with degeneration of the disc because with degenerated or weakened disc, it is easier for Nucleus pulposus to tear through Annuals fibrosus (outer part of the disc) and bulge outwards.

104

With the degeneration of disc, there are other implications as well. For example there is formation of osteophytes (bony spurs at the edge of vertebras). This further restricts the movement of the spine at that level. The facet joints in the back must be maintained at a delicate non-weight bearing relationship for their movement regulating responsibilities. A well hydrated disc brings this about by effectively packing the joint, whereas a thin disc will force these joints to become weight bearing becoming in the long run a cause for arthritis. Similarly the space for exit of nerve root (also called foramen) is also reduced with the thinning of discs and jamming of facet joints.

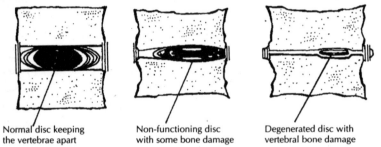

Normal disc keeping
the vertebrae apart

Non-functioning disc
with some bone damage

Degenerated disc with
vertebral bone damage

Fig. 151: Thinning and degeneration of disc

Pressure Changes on Spinal Discs

The figure shown below (Fig. 152) shows the percentage change in load acting on the lower lumbar discs with various positions of the body. The standing position is taken as the reference point and is set to zero.

Taking the upright standing intradiscal pressure as the norm, it should be noted that a five-degree tilt will increase the pressure by 25%, unsupported sitting will increase it by 50%, and lying supine decreases the pressure by 50%. By marked forward flexion and rotation, the intradiscal pressure may increase by as much as 400%. For these reasons, one can see how it is best to lift weights with a straight spine and bent knees thereby avoiding excessive forward spinal flexion.

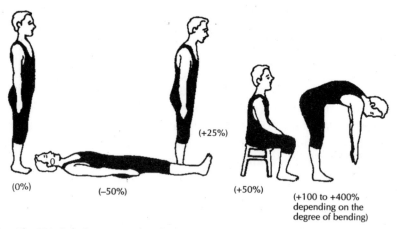

(+25%)

(0%)

(–50%)

(+50%)

(+100 to +400% depending on the degree of bending)

Fig. 152: Relative pressure on disc in various positions w.r.t. standing position

Loads most damaging to disc tissue are bending and torsional loads, especially those applied suddenly. It is observed in experiments that if spine is subjected to very high compressive load applied gradually, there is no injury to the fibres of annulus (outer part of disc) but failure of the annular fibres occurs when subjected to bending or torsional loads. It has been noticed that in case of healthy disc, even a compressive load enough to damage the body of vertebra is not sufficient to damage the disc. But, of course, when the disc becomes weak and degenerated, the condition becomes different and, in that case, the person should avoid the axial compressive loads also on the spine.

Mechanism of Slip-Disc

The otherwise tough annulus fibrosus (outerpart of disc) is somewhat weak at the back and the sides of the disc. If it gives way or gets torn, it may allow the nucleus pulposus to bulge out. If this bulge presses against one of the spinal nerves the result is pain. Infact the disc doesn't slip, it only bulges. This phenomena, in medical parlance, is also termed as Disc protrusion/Disc prolapse/Disc herniation etc. This condition normally results when there is too much pressure or lateral strain on the spine. It is usually the result of some sudden violent episodes such as a fall, an accident, sudden twisting of spine, lifting a heavy object, sudden forward bending of spine associated with lifting an object. The slip disc mostly occurs at the level of L-5 & S-1 (i.e. between 5th lumbar vertebra and 1st sacral vertebra) because this disc receives the maximum pressure and this is the point where the spine transfers the load of the upper part of body to the hip bones and thence to legs. But disc can slip at L2-L3, L3-L4 and L4-L5 level also.

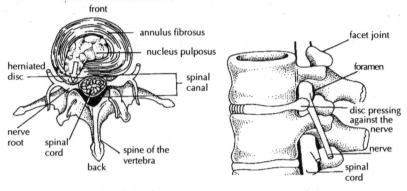

Cross-sectional view   Lateral view

Fig. 153

Fig. 154: Disc protrusion during forward bending in case of weak disc

Symptoms and Diagnosis of Slip-Disc

In addition to the pain in the lower back, the patient of slip disc also complains of pain radiating or shooting down into the back of leg (along the course of sciatic nerve which gets irritated by the pressure of disc on this nerve).

During the physical examination, the patient may not be able to raise the leg without pain (Called the 'Straight leg raising test'). Then there may be neurological changes in sensations of the legs e.g. feeling of numbness, tingling etc. There may be changes in the reflexes of knee and ankle. Then there be difference in sensations in both the legs.

One more simple and frequently used diagnostic method is to see if the fingertip pressure between the bony posterior processes of the spine or their sides produces a local pain. This is a good indication that the disc has produced soft tissue pressure on the nerve or the spinal cord which is further aggravated by a pressing of the tissue above the aggravated area.

X-ray is not sufficient diagnosis for a herniated disc. It may at best give the indication of degeneration and thinning of discs. When patient complains continuous pain in the leg and there is an increasing loss of nerve function, then a more sophisticated test known as M.R.I (Magnetic Resonance Imaging) should be got done which gives the accurate picture of the area.

Treatment of Slip Disc by Exercises

Although in the complicated cases and chronic pain, surgery is the only answer where the protruding disc is removed by surgery, but in less complicated cases the exercises mentioned below can be useful. However these exercises should be done only when the original pain is subsided by bed rest and taking analgesics or pain killers and other simple measures (e.g. heat treatment through hot water bag, heating pad, hot packs or formentation). Another precaution to be taken in exercises is that they should be done slowly without any jerks. If you find any increasing discomfort or pain by doing any exercises, discontinue that exercise. Use your intuition in this regard.

A slipped disc patient should continue to pay special emphasis on 'Good postures' as explained in chapter 2 of this book to have optimum benefit from these exercises. Forward bending should be avoided in case of slip disc.

There are mainly two types of exercises which are useful in case of Slip-disc.

1. Spine extension exercises
2. Strengthening of back and abdominal muscles

Spinal extension exercise will help to retract the disc back to its normal position. In the spinal extension exercises (backward bending) the ligaments attached to the front of the disc are stretched when the front angle is opened up. In this process, they draw the disc back into it intervertebral space and away from the nerve root or the spinal cord. At the same time, by creating a space in the position where the disc used to be, force of vacuum will be generated which sucks water for rehydration of discs and cartilage (covering the bony vertebra) enhancing its lubrication and gliding property.

The second types of exercises are mainly preventive. They serve to strengthen your back and abdominal muscles and also help in realigning the spinal vertebras in their proper axis. When the muscles of the back and abdomen have become stronger, they can easily relieve the disc of bearing excess load. Strong back and abdominal muscles support the spine better and keep the spine and pelvis in a balanced position which automatically protects the spine from injury. There is a mechanism called 'hydraulic sac mechanism' which is created by coordinated contraction of stomach muscles, back muscles, the diaphragm and pelvic floor muscles. When these muscles tighten simultaneously, the abdominal cavity which is an enclosed sac of fluid gives added support to the spine so that when the spine is called on to lift a heavy load, the total weight is not transmitted entirely through the spine. For strengthening back abdominal muscles you are requested to refer chapters 10 & 11.

Loosening exercises for relaxing tight and stiff muscles of back and hip joint also needs to be done as shown in respective chapters because with pain in the back, muscles around that region invariably remain tight. Loosening of hip joint is required because if hip joint is tight, there is more pressure on the back while bending etc. and this will worsen your slip disc problem. But only those exercises should be chosen which don't involve forward bending or if at all forward bending is to be done it should be done with knees bent. With knees bent, bending mostly takes place at hip joint and lower back is relieved from the stress. Similarly if during forward bending spine is supported by hands placed on the ground, then also there is minimal stress in lower back (see Figs. 85 & 162) because load of body is being supported by hands and legs directly and not by spine. Exercises shown in Figs. 86 to 90 are specially useful for relaxing tight back and hips.

Below are given spinal extension exercises for the relocation of slip disc.

Exercise 1

Take two big round pillows (or otherwise you can take two normal pillows in place of one big round pillow). Place them on the ground about one and a half feet apart, kneel on the pillows such that your knees rest on the rear pillows and your chest rests on front pillows and hands in front of it resting on the ground comfortably with elbows bent as shown in Fig.155. This will position your abdomen and the painful area of the back in the hollow between the pillows. Your body should be off the ground by 5 to 6″ when you lie on the pillows.

Now all that is involved is rhythmic movement of spine up and down in the hollow. When you go down. It opens up the front angle of disc spaces as shown in figures below which helps to pull the disc to its normal location.

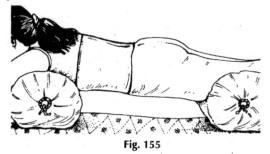

Fig. 155

Fig. 156: Position of spine representing the posture in Fig. 155

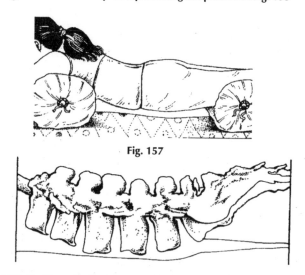

Fig. 157

Fig. 158: Position of spine representing the posture shown in Fig. 157

....

Exercise 2

Lie on your back. Bend your feet and bring them as close to your buttocks as possible keeping this position, raise your buttocks of the ground as high as possible. Remain in this position for as long as you can comfortably stay. Then come down slowly, Repeat it few times.

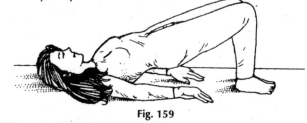

Fig. 159

....

Exercise 3

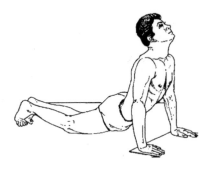

Fig. 160

Lie on your stomach. Straighten arms while inhaling. Throw chest out as far as possible. Curve backwards and look at the ceiling, stretching neck backwards to its fullest extent. In this position practically the whole weight of the body is carried by the arms.

Now reverse your body curvature. Your body should form an inverted V. Your feet should remain flat on the ground. You will feel a good stretch behind your ankle and knee in this position.

Fig. 161

Do these two positions in rhythmic movement few times. Finally come back to normal sitting/standing position kneeling on the knees and with the support of hands on the ground (see Fig. 162). Don't stand up directly.

....

Exercise 4

Fig. 162: Intermediate position

Sit in the position of Vajrasana. Inhale and then while exhaling stretch your hands ahead and bend your body forward from the buttocks (Those who feel pain in such bending needn't do it). You can put your head on the floor if you feel so. Buttocks shouldn't be raised above the heels while bending. See Fig. 85 in this book.

Now come forward gradually while keeping your hand in the same position on the ground and moving hips forward (see Fig. 162). Now inhale and bend back keeping legs and feet together. Look up and back, keeping your hips lowered.

Fig. 163: Final position

....

Exercise 5

Stand erect with feet 6" apart and parallel. Inhale, stretch your arms up and arch back from the waist pushing the hips out and keeping legs straight. Keep your hips tightened which helps in giving firm support to the lower back. Neck and head should hang back loosely looking at the ceiling. See Fig. 146 in this book.

....

Exercise 6

This exercise is nothing but what is called 'Dhanurasana' in Yoga. Lie down on your front, head down. Inhale and bend

your knees up and clasp your ankles with your hands. Inhaling, raise your head and chest up and simultaneously pull your ankles up, lifting the knees and thighs off the floor. Arch backward and look up. Then exhale and come back slowly to normal position.

Fig. 164

Those who can do chakrasana may also find it useful. But it should be done slowly without jerk. It is difficult for most of the people and hence is being omitted here. Bhujangasana and Shalbhasana shown in Figs. 137 and 138 are also very good for Slip-disc patients.

Following exercises have also been found useful in relieving the disc pressure on the nerve.

....

Exercise 7

Lie down on stomach. Lift one leg and slowly bend it with the help of hand so that the heel touches the buttock. Then follow the same process with the other leg. Then take both the legs together and bend them slowly on both the buttocks simultaneously. Remain in this position for a few minutes. In this position if you prefer you can also raise you head and chest up in this position.

Fig. 165

....

Exercise 8

Lie on your back, bend one leg and put the foot on the thigh of another leg. Now move the knee of the bent leg up and down. Do the same with the other leg.

Fig. 166

This exercise can also be done while sitting on chair (Fig. 167).

Exercise shown in Fig. 110 in this book is also useful.

Fig. 167

....

Exercise 9

Lie on a slant board with your feet elevated and anchored in the strap at the end of the board (see Fig. 145). Take your hands over your head (as in Fig. 144). In this position, your whole body including the spine is stretched with the help of gravity. It is a kind of natural traction for the spine which increases the intervertebral space and pulls the disc back freeing the nerve of its pressure. By this stretch, the spine also gets correctly aligned and any defect in its curvature tends to get rectified.

....

Exercise 10

Try dorsi flexion of your ankle joints keeping your leg straight. It stretches your entire back of leg. It can better be done by somebody else as shown in Fig.168. It helps reducing the pain of Sciatica.

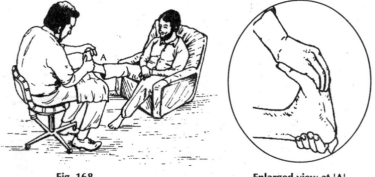

Fig. 168   Enlarged view at 'A'

Exercise shown in Fig. 142 in this book also stretches the back of leg effectively and reduces the pain of sciatica. However,

115

for doing this exercise, first you should kneel on the knee keeping spine straight and then come to this pose with the help of your hands on the ground so that no load comes on the lumbar spine. Similarly while coming back to your original posture, reverse the above sequence and never stand up suddenly.

Miscellaneous Home Remedies

Following miscellaneous treatments have also been found good for alleviating the pain of slip-disc and sciatica.

1. Massage on the back of legs: Massaging the back of legs is very effective in reducing the backache since the acupuncture meridian B1 which passes through lower back also continues in the back of leg. For massaging the back of leg, ask your patient to lie in prone position. Then work slowly up the leg starting from the ankle and right upto the hips. Use your thumbs or heels of your hands to press gradually up the muscles and flesh of calf, thigh and hips. Let your movement be continuous and rhythmic. Now a days hand rollers are also available which you can roll on the back of legs applying little pressure.

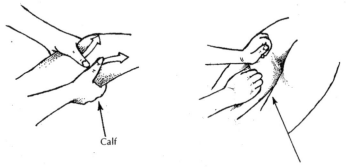

Calf

Thigh and hip

Fig. 169

There are two important acupuncture points on this meridian B1 (one at the back of knee and one in the middle of crease below the buttock) as shown in Fig. 169A. Giving intermittent pressure on these points gives substantial relief to backache.

2. Treating Spinal reflex on the foot: There is an extraordinary similarity between the shape of the spine and the shape of its reflex on the inside of the foot as shown in Figs. 170 and 171. Both have 26 bones and the four arches of the feet mirror the four curves of the spine. According to principles of 'Reflexology' if you work on the reflexes on the foot corresponding to various body parts, that body part starts healing because of the link of the reflex with that part through energy channel (or meridian). Hence if you work on the spinal reflexes on the foot, you are giving healing to your spine also. Now to work on the spinal reflexes, you start pressing at the inside edge of the heel and walk your thumb up gradually towards the big toe along the dotted line shown in the figure. For slip disc patient, the area of the spinal reflex in the foot corresponding to the lumbar curve should be given more massage.

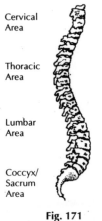

Fig. 169 A

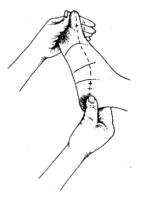

Fig. 170

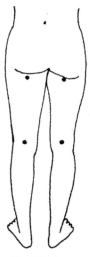

Cervical Area

Thoracic Area

Lumbar Area

Coccyx/ Sacrum Area

Fig. 171

Shape of our spine is similar to the shape of inside edge of our foot as shown in Fig. 170

Similar reflexes also exist in the hands.

3. Reiki treatment: Give Reiki to your lower back (location of Back Hara chakra) and tip of the spine at the back (Mooladhra chakra) by putting your hands as shown in Figs. 172 & 173.

Reiki at these points is more easily given in lying position. By giving Reiki here by hands, these portions are stimulated by life energy. Reiki to Mooladhra chakra is specially useful since this chakra controls the full muscular and skeletal system of the body and makes it sturdy. While giving Reiki, focus your mind also to that location. This will accelerate the healing.

(*Note:* For more details on how 'Reiki' works please refer my book **'Healing through Reiki'** from the same publisher.)

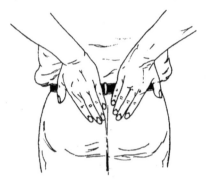

Fig. 172: Reiki to lower back or Back Hara chakra

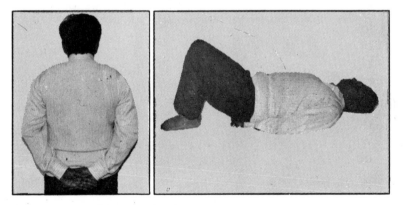

Fig. 173: Reiki to Mooladhara or Root chakra

4. Heat treatment: Heat relieves muscle spasm and bring about dilation of blood vessels thereby improving the blood supply to the affected part and consequent removal of waste products accumulated in muscles.

Heat can be given to the painful portion by a hot water bag or heating pad or by a towel soaked in hot water.

I find the following two ways most convenient for giving heat to the sore back.

(a) Lie down on your back and put hot water rubber bottle below your sacral spine. In this position heat will be going to your lumbo sacral spine while you are just lying relaxed. Moreover keeping the bottle below your sacral part of spine also causes pelvic tilt which is useful for you.

(b) Lie down in a hot water tub as shown is Fig. 174. You can also mix some salt in the water for more effectiveness.

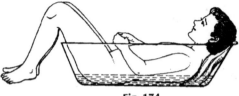

Fig. 174

5. Massage on the lower back and hips: You can also give massage to lower back in various ways to reduce pain. For example:

(a) You can apply some pain removing oil or cream on your lower back and then massage the lower back by the fingers of your hand in a clockwise circular motion.

(b) You can give pointed pressure with your thumbs on both sides of spine as shown in Fig. 175.

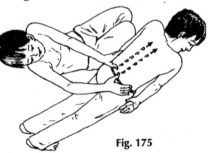

Fig. 175

(c) You can run a spine roller along the spine starting from the base of spine, by applying a little pressure.

(**Note:** Spine roller is available in market from acupressure shops.)

Massage on hips is also very effective for reducing backache in lumbar region. It can either be a simple rubbing or stroking massage as shown in Fig. 175A or hacking massage as shown

119

in Fig. 175B which is more effective. Hacking massage is given by bouncing the sides of your hands alternately and rapidly up and down with palms of both hands facing one another.

A   **B**

Fig. 175A & B

6. Pelvic tilt exercises: Pelvic tilt exercises as shown in Figs. 91 and 92 in this book should be done to correct the problems of hyperlordosis and to bring pelvis in balanced position as this is a position of least strain on the spine.

Useful Precautions for Slip-Disc Patient

Once the pain has subsided by taking various measures mentioned in this chapter, the following precautions should be taken:

1. All sports involving sudden uncontrolled movements should be avoided.

2. Any exercises which overload the back (such as aerobics) should be avoided. Swimming (especially on the back) and walking are, on the other hand, to be recommended.

3. All sporting activity must be preceded by a "warm-up".

4. Heavy weight-bearing must be avoided.

5. 'Good Postures' as given in chapter 2 of the book should invariably be maintained by a slip-disc patient to prevent undue stress on his back.

6. Asymmetrical body movements, sudden/jerky body movement and lifting of unbalanced loads w.r.t. body axis should be avoided.

7. Sudden bending and twisting should be avoided.

8. A slip disc patient should always sleep on hard bed. A thin mattress can be used over hard board or ply but thick

sagging mattress should never be used. If a thick mattress is to be used, then 'Ortho mattress' should be used which is specially designed for back patients.

9. Whenever you are on a journey where impacts and jerks are likely to be there (for example, on a rough road), always use lumbar belts (see details below).

Fig. 176

10. Avoid climbing on steep stairs and ladders as far as possible.

11. If you sit on a chair or sofa where your lower back is not· in contact with the back of seat properly, use cushion or lumbar support.(Fig. 176).

Lumbar Belt

Lumbar belt substitutes the action of your muscles. So if your back and abdominal muscles are weak, then belt can compensate for them and provide the necessary support to your spine. But one shouldn't become totally dependent on it because it will tend to further weaken your muscles. It should be used as a temporary measure only.

Fig. 177: Lumbar Belt

One should continue to strengthen his muscles by suitable exercises and strive to leave dependency on the belt at a certain point of time. When your muscles become strong they become your natural belt to support the spine.

ooo

121

Appendices

Appendix-1

Muscles associated with back

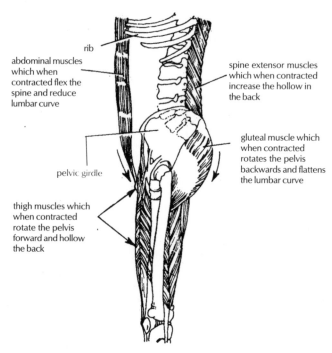

rib

abdominal muscles which when contracted flex the spine and reduce lumbar curve

spine extensor muscles which when contracted increase the hollow in the back

gluteal muscle which when contracted rotates the pelvis backwards and flattens the lumbar curve

pelvic girdle

thigh muscles which when contracted rotate the pelvis forward and hollow the back

Fig. 178

Muscles acting at hip joint

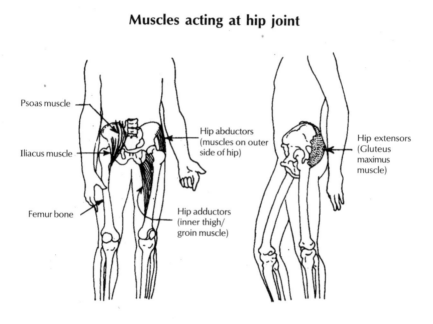

Psoas muscle

Iliacus muscle

Femur bone

Hip abductors
(muscles on outer
side of hip)

Hip adductors
(inner thigh/
groin muscle)

Hip extensors
(Gluteus
maximus
muscle)

Fig. 179

Note: Psoas and iliacus muscles together constitute hip flexors.

 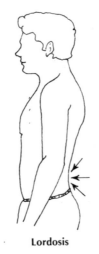 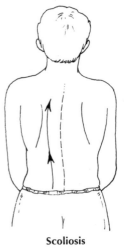

Kyphosis   Lordosis   Scoliosis

Fig. 180

Defects in Curvatures of the Spine

Kyphosis — Excessive backward curvature of the upper back

Lordosis — Excessive hollow in the lumbar spine or lower back

Scoliosis — Lateral curvature of the spine.

Muscles Associated with Neck Movement

1. Muscles causing flexion (forward bending) and rotation of your neck to the sides

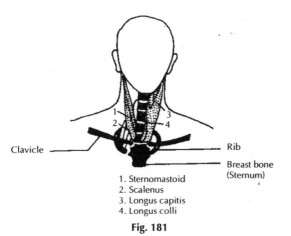

Clavicle

Rib

Breast bone
(Sternum)

1. Sternomastoid
2. Scalenus
3. Longus capitis
4. Longus colli

Fig. 181

2. Muscles causing backward bending and sideward bending

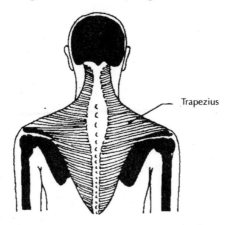

Trapezius

Fig. 182

Glossary of Terms

Anaesthetic: Drug which causes unconsciousness (general anaesthetic), or prevents pain if injected locally (local anaesthetic).

Analgesic: Pain-relieving drug.

Ankylosing spondylitis: Arthritic disease mainly of men between 20 and 40, leading to painful stiffening of spine, neck and sometimes hips and shoulders.

Cervical: of the neck.

Corticosteroids: Group of drugs acting like hormones (chemicals produced by the body) which reduce inflammation.

Crush fracture: Sudden internal 'squashing' of bone, particularly of the vertebrae.

Disc: Layer of cartilage (gristle) between vertebral bodies in spine.

Disc Protrusion: 'Slipped disc'.

Dorsal: of the middle back.

Fibrositis: Aches and pains in and around muscles of shoulders and around shoulder blades.

Foramina: Small channels in bones, for instance in cervical spine, containing nerves.

Hydrocortisone: Natural hormone made in the adrenal gland of the body; also made as a drug to swallow or inject into joints to reduce inflammation.

Kyphosis: Backward bending of spine, particularly in the dorsal region.

Lesion: Injury or disease change in organs and tissues.

Ligament: Short band of tough, flexible tissue binding bones and muscles together.

Lordosis: Forward bending of spine, particularly in the lumbar region.

Lumbar: Of the lower back.

Malignant: Applied to tumours, this means cancerous.

Neuritis: Inflammation affecting a nerve or nerves.

Osteoid osteoma: Tiny non-cancerous bone tumour.

Osteomalacia: Disease in which bones become softened; caused by lack of vitamin D in diet and lack of sunshine.

Osteoporosis: Thinning of density of bones due to ageing and other factors and often accompanied by a lack of calcium salts; common in elderly people, particularly women, often starting at the menopause (change of life).

Paget's disease: Disorder in which bones of spine, legs or skull become patchily thickened; may cause bending of long bones and skull enlargement.

Periosteum: Thin membrane around bones.

Polymyalgia rheumatica: Disease of the elderly arising from inflammation of small arteries, resulting in severe early-morning stiffness and muscle aches and pains in shoulders and hips.

Polymyositis: Inflammation of the muscles.

Prolapsed disc: Disc which has moved out of place, hence 'slipped disc'.

Rheumatoid arthritis: Chronic progressive inflammatory disease causing pain, swelling and stiffening of joints.

Rheumatology: Study of diseases which involve the joints and muscles and other structures of and around joints.

Rickets: Childhood disease of softened bones due to vitamin-D deficiency and/or too little sunshine.

Scapulae: Shoulder blades.

Sciatica: Ache or pain running down one leg from back or buttocks, due to inflammation or irritation of, or pressure on, sciatic nerve.

Scoliosis: Sideways bending of spine, *sciatic scoliosis* is sideways bending of the spine as a reaction to sciatica (see above).

Sedative: Drug which soothes and quietens nerves.

Spinal osteoarthritis: Gradual wearing and narrowing of the cartilages of the joints of the spine.

Spondylosis: Degenerative changes in spine; *cervical spondylosis* means these changes in joints between cervical vertebrae and their discs.

Spondylitis: Inflammation in the joints of the spine.

Tendon: Strong band of tissue which attaches the fleshy part of the muscle to the bone.

Thrombosis: Clotting of blood in a blood vessel.

Vertebrae: The individual bones of the spine.

Vertebral Column: 24 bony units (vertebrae) joined together with ligaments and discs to form the spine.

OOO

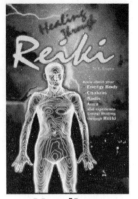

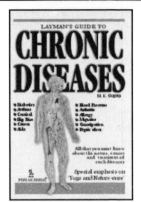

Healing Through Reiki
—M.K. Gupta

Contrary to what some people believe, Reiki is not a shady practice rooted in unfounded principles, but a systematic healing therapy based on the universal life force that pervades the entire cosmos. The Japanese refer to this invisible but universal energy as *Ki*, the Chinese as *Chi*, while Indians term it *prana*.

This energy forms an invisible pranic form around our physical body. This pranic form provides energy to the physical body and any disturbance in the pranic form affects our physical body, causing various ailments. Reiki is the science of tapping this pranic energy and using it to heal and nourish the physical body. Correcting any energy imbalance in the pranic form automatically heals the corresponding physical body.

In this book, the author highlights the association between the Japanese-discovered Reiki and the Indian healing techniques based on *chakras, nadis* and Yoga. The book also outlines Reiki attunement or the process of empowerment. With many photos and illustrations, the book reveals Reiki treatment for specific ailments.

Size: 5.5"x8.5" • *Pages: 104*
Price: Rs. 80/- • Postage: Rs. 15/-

Layman's Guide to Chronic Diseases
—M.K. Gupta

Barely a hundred years ago, the incidence of asthma, blood pressure, diabetes and cancer were low. Today, these are ranked amongst the major killer diseases. Thanks to modern lifestyles and stressful living, chronic diseases are continually on the rise. Medical science has no permanent cure for most of these diseases and simply provides short-term solutions that cause long-term complications.

Layman's Guide to Chronic Diseases provides a ray of hope through Yoga and Nature Cure. The book deals with each ailment in a scientific manner, detailing the nature of the disease and highlighting its causes. Finally, it reveals preventive and curative measures based on Yoga and Nature Cure.

This excellent self-treatment guide covers allergies, arthritis, asthma, migraine, high blood pressure, diabetes, cervical spondylosis, ulcers, cancer and the most dreaded modern disease, AIDS, besides other ailments.

Size: 5.5"x8.5" • *Pages: 176*
Price: Rs. 96/- • Postage: Rs. 15/-

Layman's Guide for HEART CARE

In simple terms, the book outlines the working of the human heart, the factors that affect it and what can go wrong. It also helps the reader gauge where he or she stands vis-à-vis heart disease. The diagnoses and various types of heart disease are dealt with subsequently. A variety of risk factors are also highlighted. These include stress, smoking and alcohol, faulty diet, obesity, sedentary lifestyles, blood pressure and diabetes, among others.

The subsequent chapters dwell on the medical treatments for heart ailments. Besides modern medical techniques, the book also tells readers about non-invasive and natural methods such as Yoga and other nature-cure alternatives.

In conclusion, the book dispels common myths surrounding this modern killer disease and enlightens readers on the true facts. Peppered with many useful charts, tables and illustrations, the book can serve as a handy guide for those suffering from heart disease or as a preventive manual for those with a family history of heart ailments.

Demy Size • Pages: 120
Price: Rs. 80/- • Postage: Rs. 15/-

HEALTH CHARTS & Tables for You

As any health-conscious person knows, health is truly wealth. Yet, simply harbouring good intentions does not ensure good health for anyone. Beginning in infancy and right up to our twilight years, a conscious attempt has to be made to lead a healthy lifestyle. In the formative years, our parents make this effort on our behalf. But as we enter the teens and take control of our own destinies, how well informed we are on health-related issues makes all the difference between physical well-being and ill health.

This book ensures you have all the facts, figures and data at your fingertips to promote proper health and nutrition in order to prevent disease.

In this book you will find: height and weight charts, blood pressure and pulse rate charts, calorie charts, fat and cholesterol charts, vitamin and mineral charts, balanced diet charts, pollution health hazard charts, infectious diseases and immunisation charts, healthy heart and stress charts... not to mention other relevant charts, tables and data.

Big Size • Pages: 144
Price: Rs. 96/- • Postage: Rs. 15/-

How to Remain Ever Free is a masterpiece by the well-known author of self-management books, Er. M.K. Gupta. This book has a vibe and style of its own which makes it completely different from the other books of this category. Once in hand, the reader flows effortlessly with the book feeling continuously the presence and vibrations of the author.

In this book, the author takes you on a journey towards freedom and happiness. According to him, freedom is the very fragrance of life. Freedom and happiness are very intimately linked with each other. However, the author makes a clear distinction between real freedom and the so called casual freedom of doing anything as per one's whims and fancies. In real freedom, one remains a master while in casual or apparent freedom, you are actually a slave or servant, though outwardly, you may appear wearing the mask of freedom.

In the present book, the author gives various tips on freedom from various negative and undesirable traits from your personality. Once negativities disappear from your being, what remains is only positivity which will give you nothing but happiness. According to the author, every human being has got both Lower nature and Higher nature in his being. When we fall towards our Lower nature, we are going towards slavery and unhappiness. Similarly, when we rise in our Higher nature, we are going towards freedom and happiness. All our negativities are a part of our Lower nature while all our positive qualities are part of our Higher nature.

Like, the author's earlier book, *How to Remain Ever Happy,* this book too is divided into small chapters with pleasing illustrations to avoid monotony while in reading the book. Further, you can read the book from anywhere as every chapter is independent and complete in itself.

Demy size • Pages: 208 • Price: Rs. 96/- • Postage: Rs. 15/-

Books on General Health & Yoga

Postage: Extra